250/150

CHRIST ABOVE ALL

AND OTHER MESSAGES

by

ROBERT G. LEE, D.D., LL.D.

ZONDERVAN PUBLISHING HOUSE
Grand Rapids   Michigan

CHRIST ABOVE ALL
Copyright 1963 by
Zondervan Publishing House
Grand Rapids, Michigan

Library of Congress Catalog Card Number 63-21172

Printed in the United States of America

CONTENTS

But all this was done, that the scriptures of the prophets might be fulfilled (Matthew 26:56).

Christ Above All

Chapter I

CHRIST ABOVE ALL

> He that cometh from above is above all . . . he
> that cometh from heaven is above all (John 3:31).

These words, stating a transcendent truth, come to us from the Holy Spirit through John the Baptist.

John the Baptist — descending upon the iniquities of his day with a torch in one hand and a sword in the other.

John the Baptist — the blood of fifteen hundred years of priests flowing in his veins.

John the Baptist — speaking mostly in judicial tones as his words were sharp arrows that pierced the hearts of prating formalists, artful hypocrites, political tricksters, skeptical Sadducees and gross materialists.

John the Baptist — bearing no credentials from the learned rabbis, exhibiting no diplomas from the schools of the prophets, never having received lessons in elocution, receiving no honorary degrees from the Jewish Sanhedrin.

John the Baptist — preaching for a verdict and getting it as is shown by multitudes who "went out to him from Jerusalem and all Judea and all the region round about Jordan, and were baptized of him in Jordan — confessing their sins" (Matthew 3:5, 6).

John the Baptist — to whom was entrusted the delicate task and sacred responsibility of interpreting the voice of betrothal as the friend of the Bridegroom.

John the Baptist — concerning whom Jesus said: "Among them that are born of women there has not risen a greater than John the Baptist" (Matthew 11:11) — concerning whom the

9

angel of the Lord spoke to Zacharias, saying: "Thou shalt call his name John . . . for he shall be great in the sight of the Lord . . . and he shall be filled with the Holy Ghost, even from his mother's womb. And many of the children of Israel shall he turn to the Lord their God" (Luke 1:13-16).

John the Baptist — seeing Jesus coming unto him, said: "Behold the Lamb of God, which taketh away the sin of the world" (John 1:29).

John the Baptist — baptizing Jesus in the rolling waters of the Jordan River, at which time the heavens were opened unto Jesus, and a voice from heaven said: "This is my beloved Son, in whom I am well pleased" (Matthew 3:16, 17).

John the Baptist — speaking these words: "He must increase, but I must decrease. He that cometh from above is above all . . . he that cometh from heaven is above all" (John 3:30, 31).

Jesus was from God, from above, from heaven. Yet some men who speak first and think afterward, who ramble without reason, who have an abundance of words but a famine of brains, say that Jesus was the product of the age in which He lived. This appears as wisdom but is ignorance. The age in which Jesus lived had not one thing to do with producing Him. Jesus, the "Plant of Renown," the "Righteous Branch," the "Rose of Sharon," the "Lily of the Valley," did not grow and was not cultivated in any earthly garden. He was "as a root out of dry ground" (Isaiah 53:2). He was not a natural product, but a supernatural *person.* He was not *produced;* He was *presented.* He was not a *production* but an *induction.* He came from above, from another world, even from heaven, and that is not production, but induction.

In the Bible we read: "The first man is of the earth, earthy: the second man is the Lord from heaven" (I Corinthians 15:47).

So that settles it. Not the product of the age in which He lived, He came from heaven *to* the age in which He lived. He came not from the loins of any man, but from the bosom of the Father. Jesus said: "I proceeded forth and came from God; neither came I of myself, but he sent me" (John 8:42). Jesus said to Nicodemus: "And no man hath ascended up to heaven, but he that came down from heaven, even the Son of man which is in heaven" (John 3:13). He also asked this question: "What and if ye see the Son of man ascend up where he was before?" (John 6:62). Jesus came down from the Father and has now gone back to the Father.

Always it is true that those who set their minds, hearts, tongues and pens to setting forth the wonders and worth of Jesus Christ set themselves to a task that would tax wise men and angels.

Though much of Christ be spoken and written in one century and still more in other centuries, eternity itself will not fully suffice to set Jesus forth as He deserves to be set forth in His greatness, His goodness, His grace, His glory. A woeful sense of inadequacy oppresses all of us as we attempt to set forth the excellencies Jesus has in Himself and the treasures of righteousness in the blood of Him "who of God is made unto us wisdom, and righteousness, and sanctification, and redemption" (I Corinthians 1:30).

Can any greatly talented musician play Beethoven's *Ninth Symphony* on a tin whistle? Can one feeble candle light the darkness of a big city? Can a bit of cheese in a mouse trap satisfy the hunger of a ravenous lion? Can one cup of water cleanse ten thousand dirty hands? Can one little coal of fire warm one hundred cold hearthstones? You say *no*. And I say no more can all the words of men most skillfully combined and most eloquently spoken set forth the life and character of Jesus Christ, whose life on earth was an episode between two eternities, one reaching back before all worlds and one forward forever.

All the words of all vocabularies cannot fully describe Jesus who was always so finely strung, so unutterably keyed to truth, mercy, justice, love — who so quickly felt the sorrow, the sympathy and the indignation which wrong and injustice invariably elicit from all high souls.

Jesus, born in denial of the laws of life and raised from the dead in defiance of the laws of death, has a name which sounds down the corridors of the centuries like the music of all choirs, visible and invisible, poured forth in one anthem. This One who came from above is today literature's loftiest ideal, philosophy's highest personality, criticism's supremest problem, theology's fundamental doctrine, spirituality's cardinal necessity. The hymn writer was not writing fiction in these words:

> No mortal can with Him compare
> Among the sons of men;
> Fairest is He than all the fair
> Who fill the heavenly train.

"He is altogether lovely" (Song of Solomon 5:16).

"He that cometh from heaven is above all."

He is heaven's bread for earth's hunger, heaven's clothing for earth's nakedness, heaven's riches for earth's poverty, heaven's water for earth's thirst, heaven's light for earth's darkness, heaven's grace for earth's guilt, heaven's gladness for earth's grief, heaven's glory for earth's shame, heaven's gain for earth's loss, heaven's love for earth's hate, heaven's wisdom for earth's follies, heaven's peace for earth's strife, heaven's hope for earth's despair, heaven's prompting for earth's perplexity, heaven's justification for earth's condemnation, heaven's comfort for earth's sorrows, heaven's cleansing for earth's dirt, heaven's salvation for earth's damnation, heaven's life for earth's death. This One had no sin *in* Him but all sin *on* Him.

Who am I to attempt to portray Jesus whom "the heaven of heavens cannot contain"? The most magnificent ceremonies assemble multitudes under the influence of Him to whom God has given a name which is above every name, and who said: "For I came down from heaven, not to do mine own will, but the will of him that sent me" (John 6:38).

> O, who can paint him? Let the sweetest tone
> That ever trembled on the harps of heaven
> Be discord. Let the enchanting seraphim
> Whose anthem is eternity, be dumb.
> For praise and wonder, adoration, all
> Melt into muteness 'ere they soar to Thee,
> The sole Perfection, Theme of countless worlds.

There never was anyone like Jesus *before* Jesus. There never has been one like Jesus *since* Jesus. There never will be another Jesus — before all, in all, all in all.

Christ Jesus is above all as to —

I. His Source

Jesus had eternal delights with His Father before the assumption of our nature, even as He created all things before His union with the seed of Abraham. Jesus could say of Himself, even as the Holy Spirit said:

> When he prepared the heavens, I was there: When he set a compass upon the face of the depth: When he established the clouds above: When he strengthened the fountains of the deep: When he gave to the sea his decree, that the waters should not pass his commandment: When he appointed the foundations of the earth: Then was I by him, as one brought up with him: and I was daily his delight, rejoicing always before him (Proverbs 8:27-30).

And Jesus *did,* in praying, say of Himself:

> And now, O Father, glorify thou me with thine own self with the glory which I had with thee before the world was (John 17:5).
> Father, I will that they also, whom thou hast given me, be with me where I am; that they may behold my glory, which thou hast given me: for thou lovedst me before the foundation of the world (John 17:24).

Meaning what — these words? Meaning that Jesus, not abased to the condition of a creature, was coexistent, coeternal, coequal, and coessential with the Father.

By the Father — the fountain and ocean and center of all delights and joys — Jesus was embraced from all eternity. Jesus said: "The Father and I are one" (John 10:30). And no wife was ever so one with the husband of her heart, no husband was ever so one with the wife of his bosom, no child ever so one with its mother from the moment of its conception, no soul ever so one with the body, as was Jesus with God the Father in the glory and love they had with each other and for each other before the world was. No beams of light ever came so brightly from the sun, no fragrance ever issued so sweetly from flowers, no crystal streams ever came so clearly from crystal fountains as did the delights of the holy, holy, holy Father's heart in embrace with the thrice-holy Son in the glory and love they had with and for each other before the world was — from which glory and love the blessed Holy Spirit Himself was never excluded. "I was daily his delight, rejoicing always before him" — an infinite rejoicing, suitable to the infinite perfection and holiness of the divine Being.

Christ, the Alpha and Omega, the beginning and the end, is above all in —

II. His Relation to Creation

This material universe, considered one way, is a vast autograph album — with its pages made up of mountains, molecules, motes, atoms, islands, seas, rivers, forests and plains. But the signature of Christ Jesus is found everywhere — sometimes so small you have to have a microscope to see and read it, sometimes so large, and yet being so far away man has to journey a billion miles on a telescopic lens to see and read it.

Creation in concept is the product of His wisdom. Creation in mystery and perfection is the product of His power. In the Bible, we read: "All things were made by him: and without him was not any thing made that was made" (John 1:3). "The world was made by him" (John 1:10). ". . . God, who created all things by Jesus Christ" (Ephesians 3:9).

> For by him were all things created, that are in heaven, and that are in earth, visible and invisible, whether they be thrones, or dominions, or principalities, or powers: all things were created by him, and for him: And he is before all things, and by him all things consist. And he is the head of the body, the church: who is the beginning, the firstborn from the dead; that in all things he might have the preeminence (Colossians 1:16-18).
> God, who at sundry times and in divers manners spake in time past unto the fathers by the prophets, Hath in these last days spoken unto us by his Son, whom he hath appointed heir of all things, by whom also he made the worlds (Hebrews 1:1, 2).

"Unto the Son he saith . . . . the heavens are the works of thine hands" (Hebrews 1:8, 10). "Thou art worthy, O Lord, to receive glory and honour, and power: for thou hast created all things, for thy pleasure they are and were created" (Revelation 4:11).

These words are clearly addressed to the slain Lamb of chapters five and six.

We read of an angel:

> And the angel which I saw stand upon the sea and upon the earth lifted up his hand to heaven, And sware by him that liveth for ever and ever, who created heaven, and the things that therein are, and the earth, and the things that therein are, and the sea, and the things which are therein (Revelation 10:5, 6).

Dr. Pickering tells us that in 1905, Dr. Darwin, nephew of Charles Darwin, closed his presidential address on "The Riddle of the Universe" to the Royal Society in Cape Town with these remarkable words: "After all the riddle of the universe *remains* unread." Had these men of renown been sensible and read the Bible, they would have found these words that solve the riddle: "Through faith we understand that the worlds were framed by the word of God, so that things which are seen were not made of things which do appear" (Hebrews 11:3).

We agree with the noble Dr. Pickering when he writes: "That salvation which has held the field for ages, holds it today — and when Darwin and his discredited theory of Evolution are no more, it will be admitted as the true and only salvation — God spake, worlds were." And in our confused and chaotic day, Jesus, the creating power and person, is at the center, the circumference, and all intervening spaces, upholding all things by the word of his power.

Thinking upon this, we ask: Who poured out from the crystal chalices the Amazon, the Po, the Volga, the Rhine, the Nile, the Mississippi and all other rivers of the world? Who painted the first flowers and fringed them with celestial beauty and filled them with heavenly fragrance? Who put the sun yonder in his tabernacle in the heavens — making "as a bridegroom coming out of his chamber, and rejoiceth as a strong man to run a race"? (Psalm 19:5).

Who took clots of the sun's red blood and turned them into diamonds? Who planted the moon in the garden of the stars, making it to blossom at the full like a huge jonquil in a public garden? Who sent out the first ray of light like some flaming archangel with garments afire across the uncharted dark? Who made Eden's boughs to be emerald harps on which the winds played resurrection melodies? Who first lit the world house with planet lamps and star flambeaus? Who bound "the sweet influence of the Pleiades and loosed the bands of Orion"? Who gendered "the hoary frost of heaven"? Who put the song in the throat of the mockingbird — the Beethoven of the boughs? Who put the lyric in the throat of the lark — the Mendelssohn of the meadows? Who put the treasures in the bosom and bowels of old Mother Earth?

There is one name only that answers all these questions — "*Jesus.*" We say, with Isaiah:

> Lift up your eyes on high, and behold who hath created these things, that bringeth out their host by number: he calleth them all by names by the greatness of his might, for that he is strong in power; not one faileth (Isaiah 40:26).

Again, Christ Jesus is above all in the way in which He was —

III. Made Flesh

> In the beginning was the Word, and the Word was with God, and the Word was God. The same was in the beginning with God (John 1:1, 2).
> And the Word was made flesh, and dwelt among us, (and we beheld his glory, the glory as of the only begotten of the Father,) full of grace and truth (John 1:14).
> Concerning his Son Jesus Christ our Lord, which was made of the seed of David according to the flesh (Romans 1:3).

In eternity, Jesus Christ rested on the bosom of the Father without a mother. In time, Jesus rested on the bosom of a mother without an earthly father. An uncreated divine person, who had eternal pre-existence, He took the form of a created Being and became in time what He was not in eternity —*flesh* —

the omnipotent and omniscient Creator born of the creature woman. God who, in Eden's garden, took from the body of man a motherless woman, in Bethlehem's barn brought a fatherless man from the body of a woman, and Jesus, the Ancient of Days, became the infant of days — a baby just as old as the Heavenly Father and ages older than His earthly mother.

The superlative unique, the great unlike is Jesus — "the Desire of all nations." Jesus who made man "was made in the likeness of men" (Philippians 2:7). Jesus, who created angels was made lower than heaven's angels (Colossians 1:16; Hebrews 2:7).

Jesus who said: "Before Abraham was, I am," was born two thousand years after Abraham (John 8:52-58). Jesus who was David's son was David's Lord, and Abraham's Seed was Abraham's Saviour (Matthew 22:42-45; John 8:56). Jesus who was "clothed with honour and majesty" (Psalm 104:1), was "wrapped in swaddling clothes" (Luke 2:12). Jesus, who created flesh, was "made flesh." *When* was Jesus "made flesh"? At that holy time when a Jewish virgin who had never known a man, who had never touched a man, made holy journey into that mysterious land of motherhood and came back holding in her arms the *only* baby who never had an earthly father. And His every muscle was a pulley divinely swung, His every nerve divine handwriting, His every bone divine sculpture, His every heartbeat divine pulsation, His every breath the whisper of deity. This baby was God's will, God's purpose, God's thought swathed in mortality. He was the Light — God *seen*. He was the Word — God *heard*. He was the Life — God *felt*.

Milton beautifully and appropriately wrote of Christ, the God-man, our infinite God "made flesh," in these words:

> That glorious form, that Light insufferable,
> That far-beaming blaze of majesty
> Wherewith He was wont at Heaven's high council table
> To sit in the midst of tribal unity,
> He laid aside — and here, with us to be,
> Forsook the courts of everlasting day,
> And chose with us a darksome house of clay.

The Incarnation of the Son of God is the *fact* of God's becoming man. The virgin birth is the *method* by which God the

Son became man. The *fact* of the Incarnation lies in the ever existing God putting aside His glory to become man. The method of the Incarnation is the *manner* by which He chose to come, namely, the miraculous conception in the womb of the virgin who knew not any man until she had brought forth the first born Son. "And the word was made flesh, and dwelt among us, (and we beheld his glory, the glory as of the only begotten of the Father,) full of grace and truth" (John 1:14). Thus did Jesus come from the infinite position of eternal Godhead to the finite limitations of manhood.

Christ is above all as the —

IV. REVELATION OF GOD

> No man hath seen God at any time; the only begotten Son, which is in the bosom of the Father, he hath declared him (John 1:18).

We read:

> If ye had known me, ye should have known my Father also: and from henceforth ye know him, and have seen him. Philip saith unto him, Lord, shew us the Father, and it sufficeth us. Jesus saith unto him, Have I been so long time with you, and yet hast thou not known me, Philip? he that hath seen me hath seen the Father; and how sayest thou then, Shew us the Father? (John 14:7-9).
>
> His dear Son . . . . Who is the image of the invisible God, the firstborn of every creature (Colossians 1:13, 15).

These words declare that Jesus was infinite, for nothing less than infinity can reveal God. Whoever *reveals* God must *be* God. Jesus expressed the entire being of God with entire precision, with utter finality, with unquestioned perfection. In Jesus the silence of God breaks into full voice. For us to know Jesus is to know God. And what Jesus was to prodigal and publican, to mother and child, to harlot and hypocrite, to saint and sinner, to rich and poor, to devils and disciples, to soldiers and scholars, to peasants and philosophers, to kings and beggars, that is God always and everywhere to all people in all climes.

All that God is in Christ is fully revealed. Preciously wealthy the words — for us today:

And all things are of God, who hath reconciled us to himself by Jesus Christ, and hath given to us the ministry of reconciliation; to wit, that God was in Christ, reconciling the world unto himself, not imputing their trespasses unto them; and hath committed unto us the word of reconciliation (II Corinthians 5:18, 19).

Jesus was the mind of God — thinking out. Jesus was the heart of God — throbbing out. Jesus was the hands of God — reaching out. Jesus was the feet of God — walking out. Jesus was the eyes of God — looking out. Jesus was the ears of God — listening out. Jesus was the person of God in human clothes.

In Jesus, divine omnipotence moved in a human arm. In Jesus, divine wisdom was cradled in a human brain. In Jesus divine love throbbed in a human heart. In Jesus, divine compassion glowed in human eyes. In Jesus, divine grace poured forth in human lips.

The character of Jesus is the *all* of God. Being God, without beginning, without mutation, beyond measure and without end. No other being, other than God, can claim equality with Jesus Christ. Jesus is God above all, in all, through all, the Almighty.

As somebody, whose name I forget, wrote, Christ Jesus expressed: "The friendly affinity of fatherly authority, The devout integrity of divine immutability, The generous legacy of glorious liberality, The humble courtesy of holy constancy, The manifold ministry of majestic mercy, The wealthy sympathy of worthy sublimity, The healthy sanctity of heavenly sincerity, The manifest majesty of mediative mystery."

Jesus is no mere "emanation," "effulgence," "likeness," "symbol," "reflection" of God, but *is* God, *was* God, and *will ever be* God — "blessed forevermore."

Today's health may be tomorrow's sickness, today's wealth may be tomorrow's poverty, and today's happy companionship of joy may be tomorrow's aching solitude of heart, but today's Christ is tomorrow's Christ — "the same yesterday, today, and forever" (Hebrews 13:8).

Now think of Christ above all in —

V. Supernatural Power

Jesus, who had power over all flesh (John 17:2), who amazed people in manifesting the mighty power of God (Luke 9:43), who astonished people when He spoke with words of power (Luke 4:32), who had power to lay down His life and power to take it up again (John 10:18), said: "All power is given unto me in heaven and in earth" (Matthew 28:18)

In power, Jesus is above and beyond all the forces and facts of nature as a river is beyond a rill in reach, as a tornado is above and beyond a zephyr in the movement of objects, as the sun is beyond a candle in brightness, as the Niagara Falls are beyond a mud hole in beauty. And for lessening the sum of human anguish and in lightening loads and brightening roads for people, Jesus met blind men and gave them sight, dumb men and enabled them to speak, crippled men and enabled them to walk, deaf men and made them hear. Jesus met devil-possessed men and rid them of the devils. He met lepers and cleansed them. He met crazy men and restored their minds. He met outcast women and lifted them up and back into the path of virtue. He went into rooms where the sick languished and made them well. He went into cemeteries and raised the dead. He met funeral processions and broke them up. Jesus, a miracle greater than all His miracles, wrought miracles. Thus Jesus is the undeniable testimony to the truth that all power was, and is, His in heaven and in earth.

Christ is no glorified bellhop running up and down the corridors of His world hotel — having lost the keys to some of the doors. Christ Jesus is no superannuated butler in His own world house. He is no law-limited Christ.

Though many educators seek to play Jesus' deity down to the level of human "divinity," though numerous organized efforts seek to revile and discredit Jesus, though many present-day functionaries are arrayed against His Saviourhood and Lordship, no personality at present so grips the human thought, and so dominates, so controls, and so consumes the human soul as the personality of Jesus. While modernistic and agnostic thinkers, with H. G. Wells, agree that Christ, historically speaking, should be placed upon the topmost rung of the ladder, yet, orthodox Christians, at present controlling occidental social orders, consistently claim that the incomparable works of Christ are not products simply of a historical personality, a maker of history, or a doer of deeds, but the nature of His activities places Him in a class all to Himself.

No wonder William Edward Lecky, the Irish enthusiastic historian of rationalism, wrote concerning Christ in "the days of his flesh": "The simple record of three short years of active life has done more to regenerate and soften mankind than all the disquisitions of philosophers and all the exhortations of moralists."

Christ was above all in His —

VI. TEACHINGS

Teacher of teachers was Jesus.

We read:

> So there was a division among the people because of him. And some of them would have taken him; but no man laid hands on him. Then came the officers to the chief priests and Pharisees; and they said unto them, Why have ye not brought him? The officers answered them, Never man spake like this man (John 7:43-46).

What a difference in the doctrines of Plato, Sophocles, Aristides, Socrates, Aristotle, and the doctrines of Jesus, who stands out above all teachers as a great palm tree in a desert of mediocrity. You feel the difference in the doctrines of all philosophers and the doctrine of Jesus as the difference between inquiry and declaration, the difference between speculation and revelation, between groping and guidance, between surmise and certainty, between man's little teacup mind and God's oceanic mind. Yea, the difference between the lark's sweet lyric and the parrot's raucous squawk, between the brook's shallow babble and the deep river's quiet flow.

In boldness of conception, in grandeur of character, in sublimity of purpose, in originality of mind, in valiant propagandism, Jesus' teachings claim the sovereignty of the world.

Jesus said: "We speak that we do know" (John 3:11). Leaving behind Him no interrogation marks, giving the humble virtues crowns of gold, making alien skies friendly, keeping warm and sympathetic hands on practical life, teaching men how to die unto self and unto the world and yet master both, Jesus, as a Teacher, dwells apart in His unrivaled genius. The sayings, the ethics, the doctrines promulgated by Jesus, the lowly Nazarene, have so gripped men's consciences, touched men's hearts, and fired men's imaginations that, like huge stones dropped into a vast pool, eddying it to its utmost bounds, Jesus' teachings have eddied and eddied throughout all times and throughout all climes, until they have reached the farthest corners of the utmost continents. Take away His doctrines from the literature and languages of the libraries of nations, and mostly empty shelves would remain.

Today, when the air is troubled with doubts, thick with negations that have no mission and no adventure and no beneficent audacities, we need to examine the teachings of Jesus — teachings which spurned the established boundaries of His day, leap across conventional gulfs and deep chasms which yawn between race and race, class and mass, sex and sex, sects and sects.

We need to consider His doctrines in the light of what God spoke on the Mount of Transfiguration: "This is my beloved Son, in whom I am well pleased. Hear ye Him." Hear Jesus and not men. Hear Jesus and not philosophers. Hear Jesus and not the mental rummagings of men. Hear Jesus whose every doctrine was, and is, a palace of hope.

Hear Jesus! His teaching builds palaces upon the graves of slain passions. Hear Jesus! His teaching exalts defeat into stepping-stones to a larger faith. Hear Jesus! His teachings show us how to find life by losing life, to multiply by dividing, to increase by diminishing, to live by dying.

Christ Jesus is above all in His —

VII. SACRIFICE AND SUFFERING

"Christ our Passover is sacrificed for us" (I Corinthians 5:7). At the dedication of the glorious Temple in Jerusalem animal sacrifices were made — sacrifices great as to number.

Concerning the bringing of the Ark of the Covenant and the holy vessels of the Tabernacle into the Temple, we read:

> And they brought up the ark, and the tabernacle of the congregation, and all the holy vessels that were in the tabernacle, these did the priests and the Levites bring up. Also king Solomon, and all the congregation of Israel that were assembled unto him before the ark, sacrificed sheep and oxen, which could not be told nor numbered for multitude (II Chronicles 5:5, 6).

Concerning the dedication of the Temple, we read:

> Then the king and all the people offered sacrifices before the Lord. And king Solomon offered a sacrifice of twenty and two thousand oxen, and an hundred and twenty thousand sheep: so the king and all the people dedicated the house of God (II Chronicles 7:5, 6).

But above and beyond these blood sacrifices was the sacrifice when Jesus shed His blood on Golgotha.

> Not all the blood of beasts
> On Jewish altars slain
> Could give the guilty conscience peace
> Or wash away the stain.
> But Christ, the heavenly Lamb,
> Takes all our sins away —
> A sacrifice of nobler name
> And richer blood than they.

Great the Gospel of Christ's revealing truth. Wonderful the Gospel of Christ's saving power and condescending comradeship. But greater is the Gospel of Christ's measureless sacrifice.

Once, after I had preached the baccalaureate sermon at the Northwestern Theological Seminary, the graduating class wanted an interview with me. The interview granted, these young people asked me many questions. One unusual question asked was this one: "If you had to pick out just one verse in the Bible to set forth the meaning of Christ's cross and His suffering, which verse would you choose?"

I picked this verse:

For he hath made him to be sin for us, who knew no
sin; that we might be made the righteousness of God
in him (II Corinthians 5:21).

What meaneth these words? They mean that in His sacrifice
and sufferings on Calvary's cross, Christ Jesus became for us all
that God must judge that we, through faith in Him, may become all that God cannot judge — that on Golgotha Jesus, the
perfectly righteous One, was judged as unrighteous that we, the
unrighteous ones, through faith in Him, may be judged as
righteous. They mean that on Calvary, Jesus, nailed naked to
the cross, stood before God with all our sins upon Himself that
we, through repentance toward God and faith in Jesus, may
stand before God with none of our sins upon ourselves. The
words mean that God ordered sin to execution in the person of
Jesus — dealing with Jesus as He must deal with sin, in severe
and unrelenting judgment.

What measureless suffering and sacrifice by Jesus who was
human and divine — sinless man and holy God in one person.

But there was more than the human nature in Christ which
suffered. Had it been no more than His human nature which
suffered, He would have suffered only finite suffering. If only
the human nature of Jesus suffered, and suffered only a short
time, we can not say that His sufferings were infinite. And if
His sufferings were not infinite, they could not be a satisfaction
for our sins, which sins demand infinite suffering. If the divine
nature did not suffer in its union with the human nature, then
a suffering and sacrificial Saviour is no revelation of the nature
of God. If only the human nature suffered, and that suffering
was not participated in by the divine nature, we have an infinite
debt of sin canceled by finite suffering, which is absurd. With
only a finite price paid, our salvation can not merit endless
renown.

By His back cut to shreds and to the bone with Pilate's merciless
scourge, by His face beaten into a pulp and some of His beard
pulled out, by the dirty sputum that befouled His face, by the
thorns that punctured His brow, by the hard hands that blind-

folded Him and slapped Him, by the bloody sweat of Gethsemane's garden, by His death couch of wood with four spikes,
two for the hands and two for the feet, I can say that Jesus'
suffering was the suffering of His soul. By physical and soul
suffering — His body and soul both in torture — Jesus paid our
staggering sin debt.

We are told in the Bible that the pangs of hell gat hold upon
Jesus:

> The sorrows of death compassed me, and the pains of
> hell gat hold upon me: I found trouble and sorrow
> (Psalm 116:3).

Dr. B. H. Carroll, whose mind put down beside some theological minds of our day would be as a reservoir put down beside
a teacup, said:

"It is unquestionable that Christ's soul entered hell while he
was on the cross. 'The pangs of hell gat hold upon me' (Psalm
116:3). He died the spiritual death when He said: 'My God,
My God, why hast Thou forsaken me?' And the devil and
demons were around Him. And the thirst of hell was upon Him.
But 'his soul was not left in hell' (Acts 2:31). He was there.
But He was not there to stay. He came out of hell to say to
the Father: 'Receive my spirit.' He was no longer forsaken of
the Father. Christ's descent into hell was during the three hours
of darkness when He was God-for-saken and in the power of
Satan."

"Jesus Paid It *All*." If Jesus did not pay *all* this debt penalty,
and we are required to pay the unpaid part, then Christ is only a
co-redeemer with ourselves, and not a full and absolute Redeemer
— an absurdity that pleases Satan and displeases God. But,
thanks be unto God, there is no weakness or insufficiency in
His surety.

> Forasmuch as ye know that ye were not redeemed with
> corruptible things, as silver and gold, from your vain
> conversation received by tradition from your fathers;
> But with the precious blood of Christ, as of a lamb with-
> out blemish and without spot: Who verily was fore-
> ordained before the foundation of the world, but was
> manifest in these last times for you (I Peter 1:18-20).

How grateful this should make us all — obedient to these words:

> For ye are bought with a price: therefore glorify God in your body, and in your spirit, which are God's (I Corinthians 6:20).
> Ye are bought with a price; be not ye the servants of men. Brethren, let every man, wherein he is called, therein abide with God (I Corinthians 7:23, 24).

Consider now how Christ is above all in His —

VIII. RELATION TO DEATH

Paul, by the Holy Spirit, wrote:

> For I delivered unto you first of all that which I also received, how that Christ died for our sins according to the scriptures; And that he was buried, and that he rose again the third day according to the scriptures (I Corinthians 15:3, 4).

Christ died — on a death couch of hard wood and cruel spikes. Thorns His pillow. Nakedness His covering. Vinegar and gall His deathbed drink. Derisions mocking His agonies. Voices in reviling, hoots His only inaugural acclaim. Midnight coming down at midday and pushing noonday with her brightly resplendent garments off the throne of the universe. Blood dripping. The earth groaning in convulsive earthquake throbs. Rocks — less hard than men's hearts — rending. Dice, thrown by gamblers, rattling. Soldiers guffawing. Lover and friend "standing aloof from his sore" (Psalm 38:11).

Yes. And He was buried.

The kingdom about which He had talked had shrunk to the narrow dimensions of a grave. The regal robes they had hoped to see Him wear were now a shroud. The throne they had hoped to see Him occupy had disappeared in a tomb. His only scepter — a weed. His only crown — a crown of thorns. His only coronation acclamation — the spit they flung through sneering lips. His only throne — a cross. His only emblem of royal insignia — the marks of the scourge upon His naked back. His only inaugural speech — a lonely cry. His only glory — shame. His only coronation companions — two thieves. His only inaugural splendor — the black darkness that shrouded the world. His only king's cup — the sponge filled with vinegar and gall. His only authority — His failure to come down from the cross.

Death, whose only flowers are faded garlands on coffin lids, had trampled into lifeless dust the Rose of Sharon. *Death,* whose only music is the sob of broken hearts, had padlocked the mouth that so comfortingly had spoken to the sad. *Death,* whose only pleasure fountains are the falling tears of the world, had closed the eyes of Him who wept over Jerusalem. *Death,* with skeleton hand, had written "Ichabod" on all His claims. He arose — "arose a victor from the dark domain."

> And if Christ be not risen, then is our preaching vain, and your faith is also vain. Yea, and we are found false witnesses of God . . . And if Christ be not raised, your faith is vain; ye are yet in your sins. Then they also which are fallen asleep in Christ are perished. If in this life only we have hope in Christ, we are of all men most miserable (I Corinthians 15:14, 15, 17-19).

Yes. 'Tis true. If Christ be not risen, death mocks our hopes like a coarse comedian or a heartless satirist. No risen Christ, the whole history of Christianity and its existence is unintelligible. No risen Christ, the whole earth in deepest mourning dressed, will, like Rachel of old, go down to the Judgment weeping for her children — finding no comfort.

But, in relation to death, we find some words that testify that Christ is above all, namely:

> But now is Christ risen from the dead, and become the firstfruits of them that slept (I Corinthians 15:20).
> I am he that liveth, and was dead; and, behold, I am alive for evermore, Amen; and have the keys of hell and of death (Revelation 1:18).

So we have a Christ alive — no mere shadow Christ of legend and myth, no hypothetical Christ of sentimental conjuring, no imminent Christ of nature, no pale Christ of historical imagination, no mere dream Christ of culture and romance, no mere heroic Christ of the poet's imagination, no mere artistic Christ

other religions Buda, mohamed, Luthern

of the painter's conception, no cold marble Christ of the sculptor's chisel, no mere ivory Christ on a crucifix, no dead-figure Christ of a creedal sacophagus, no mere eulogized Christ of the orator's post-morten rhetoric, no apparition Christ of yesterday, no coffined Christ of the embalmer's art. But a Christ alive — offering the inexhaustible fountains of His strength, freshening and vitalizing the hidden mysteries of our own being.

Let us remember, too, that Christ is above all in His —

IX. CERTAIN RETURN TO EARTH

"I will come again," says Jesus.

"In such an hour as ye think not, the Son of man cometh" (Matthew 24:44).

> And when he had spoken these things, while they beheld, he was taken up; and a cloud received him out of their sight. And while they looked stedfastly toward heaven as he went up, behold, two men stood by them in white apparel; Which also said, Ye men of Galilee, why stand ye gazing up into heaven? this same Jesus, which is taken up from you into heaven, shall so come in like manner as ye have seen him go into heaven (Acts 1:9-11).
>
> For the Lord himself shall descend from heaven with a shout, with the voice of the archangel, and the trump of God: and the dead in Christ shall rise first: then we which are alive and remain shall be caught up together with them in the clouds, to meet the Lord in the air: and so shall we ever be with the Lord. Wherefore comfort one another with these words (I Thessalonians 4:16-18).

The personal, literal, bodily, visible return of Christ Jesus to this earth is the central and controlling event of the future. Christ's own personal return is the supreme event — and it is bound up indissolubly with the things which precede and the events which follow. The center of the Christian hope is in the return of Jesus. And in that blessed day His feet shall stand again upon the Mount of Olives — as when, marred and scarred with the stigmata of the cross, His feet were lifted in ascension power.

> And his feet shall stand in that day upon the mount of Olives, which is before Jerusalem on the east, and the

> mount of Olives shall cleave in the midst thereof toward
> the east and toward the west, and there shall be a very
> great valley; and half of the mountain shall remove to-
> ward the north, and half of it toward the south (Zech-
> ariah 14:4).

And when Jesus does come back, His Second Advent will be
the watchman's looked-for day, the husbandman's harvest day,
the builder's completion day, the master's reckoning day, the
servant's payday, the king's coronation day, the bride's wedding
day.

> He which testifieth these things saith, Surely I come
> quickly. Amen. Even so, come, Lord Jesus (Revelation
> 22:20).

No wonder that men have testified that Christ Jesus is the
central, supreme, and superlative fact of the ages.

Joseph Ernest Renan, whose *Vie de Jesus* is recognized as the
infidel record, wrote: "All history is incomprehensible without
Christ. He is the incomparable Man. To tear His name from
the world would rend it to its foundations."

Jean Jacques Rousseau, famous and infamous French writer
and infidel, wrote: "The life and death of Jesus are those of
a God."

Immanuel H. Fichte, German philosopher and altruist, wrote:
"Till the end of time, all the sensible will bow before Jesus of
Nazareth, and will humbly acknowledge the exceeding glory
of this great phenomenon. His followers are nations and
generations."

David Frederick Strauss, author of many attacks on Christ
and Christianity, wrote: "Christ stands alone and unapproached
in the world's history."

And now, finally, we would ask —

X. Some Questions

Where have you, as an individual for whom Christ died,
placed this glorious Christ whom God hath highly exalted and
hath given a name which is above every name? Have you given

Christ Jesus highest place — a place above everybody and everything?

Are you putting family above Jesus?

Are you putting business, pleasure, personal ambition, friends, ahead of Jesus?

Are you placing self, your self, above Him?

Are you letting anybody or anything keep you from giving Jesus highest place in your life?

Do you, refusing Christ supremacy in your body, give Jesus place above all in the use of your talents?

Do you give Him minutes of service when you could give Him hours? — hours instead of days? — a year or so when you should give Him a whole lifetime?

Where do you place Jesus in your love life?

Where do you place Jesus in the use of your body, which God urges you to present to Him, along with all the body's members, as instruments of righteousness unto God?

Some are putting family ahead of Jesus. Are you?

Some are putting business ahead of Jesus. Are you?

Some are putting pleasure ahead of Jesus. Are you?

Some are putting friends ahead of Jesus. Are you?

Some are putting themselves ahead of Jesus. Are you?

Let me ask you to put Jesus above everything and everybody. Stick not to the transient things of this world — as some who foolishly prefer sound to substance.

Have no infatuation with this world — with its stagnant waters.

Have no ears for the world's broken harps. Drink not the world's chalices cracked at the world's dry wells.

Have no friendship with this world — because "the friendship with this world is enmity with God. Whosoever, therefore, will be a friend of the world is the enemy of God" (James 4:4).

God said of Abraham: "My friend."

So place Jesus above all in your life that God can speak of you as He spoke of Abraham.

Redemption by Christ

Chapter II

REDEMPTION BY CHRIST

> In whom we have redemption through his blood, the forgiveness of sins, according to the riches of his grace (Ephesians 1:7).
> In whom we have redemption through his blood, even the forgiveness of sins (Colossians 1:14).
> But of him are ye in Christ Jesus, who of God is made unto us wisdom, and righteousness, and sanctification, and redemption (I Corinthians 1:30).
> Thou . . . . hast redeemed us to God by thy blood out of every kindred, and tongue, and people, and nation (Revelation 5:9).

"Redemption" is a greater word than "creation." It is a river, not a rill, in God's language. It is an ocean, not a pond, in God's manifestations of mercy. It is an organ whose full breath is thunder, not a flute giving forth dawdling ditties in the expressed evidence of God's great love for sinners.

There are three Greek words translated "redeem" in the New Testament. One means to go into the market place to buy a captive. Another word means to bring out of the market place that which is bought. The third word means to set free, to let go — after it is bought. It requires all three words to tell the whole story of sin, bondage and redemption.

In the New Testament the word "redemption," or "salvation," refers to the entire work of Jesus in delivering us from the guilt, the penalty, the power, the presence, the consequences of sin. It is a comprehensive term and includes, in its fullest sense, justification, regeneration, sanctification, healing, resurrection, adoption, glorification. It is like a volume in one word — all organs in one diapason.

Note the —

I. NEED OF REDEMPTION

Sin undermined the constitutional order of man's nature, threw him woefully deranged, miserable, erratic, lost in interminable leagues of night. Man's sinful nature has made man captive, held man in bitter bondage. Consequently, men need to "recover themselves out of the snare of the devil, who are taken captive by him at his will" (II Timothy 2:26).

The prophet Hosea said: "O Israel, thou hast destroyed thyself" (Hosea 3:9). All the captivity that Israel knew was because of sin — the seed big with future pain and grief.

The human race for ages, even as now it is, has been in bondage to the *power* of sin. Hence, sins are called chains, fetters, bonds, galling yokes. The power of sin is called the law of sin and death. The human race, since Adam and Eve lost Eden, has been, even as now it is, in bondage to the *punishment* of sin. Hence, the sinner's heart is naturally full of fear. The Philistine enemies of the souls of men are upon sinners — seeking to blind and bind and grind them as they did Samson. The devil, with power to transform himself into an angel of light (II Corinthians 11:14), "the prince of the power of air" (Ephesians 2:2), who lied to Eve and caused the fall of man (Genesis 3), who tempted Christ (Matthew 4:3-10), who entered into Judas Iscariot (Luke 22:3), and into Ananias (Acts 5:3), who perverts the Scripture (Matthew 4:6), who opposes God's work (Zechariah 3:1), who hinders the Gospel (Matthew 13:19), who works lying wonders (II Thessalonians 2:9), who is the father of liars (John 8:44), who is presumptuous, proud, powerful, wicked, malignant, subtle, deceitful, fierce and cruel, for whom everlasting fire is prepared (Matthew 25:41) — this is he who is upon sinners — seeking whom he may devour.

This malicious enemy of men acts first like a creeping serpent and then like a flying dragon — deceiving men with all the rhetoric hell can invent, always using a phraseology that lends respectability to sin. The wrath of God is upon impenitent sinners — and His favor has departed from all unbelievers.

He that believeth on him is not condemned: but he that believeth not is condemned already, because he hath not believed in the name of the only begotten Son of God (John 3:18).

He that believeth on the Son hath everlasting life: and he that believeth not the Son shall not see life; but the wrath of God abideth on him (John 3:36).

Miserable is the condition of every man by nature. Men are by nature children of wrath (Ephesians 2:3).

Dwight Moody repeatedly said: "By nature we are a bad lot." Man is, by nature, a self-chained Prometheus — and the vultures that feed on his vitals are of his own hatching. The fire that burns him is of his own kindling. The thorny bed, with pillows of stone, is of his own making. The hairy garments that bring such discomfort, are of his own weaving — because all are born in and under sin.

Job asks:

What is man, that he should be clean? and he which is born of a woman, that he should be righteous? Job 15:14).

How then can man be justified with God? or how can he be clean that is born of a woman? (Job 25:4).

What David said, we must all say: "Behold, I was shapen in iniquity; and in sin did my mother conceive me" (Psalm 51:5). Paul, stating that "both Jews and Gentiles are all under sin (Romans 3:9), states:

There is none that understandeth, there is none that seeketh after God. They are all gone out of the way, they are together become unprofitable; there is none that doeth good, no, not one. Their throat is an open sepulchre; with their tongues they have used deceit; the poison of asps is under their lips: Whose mouth is full of cursing and bitterness: their feet are swift to shed blood: Destruction and misery are in their ways; And the way of peace have they not known: There is no fear of God before their eyes (Romans 3:11-18).

Sin deposes God from His sovereignty, abuses God's goodness, abhors God's holiness, villifies God's wisdom, insults and denies God's omniscience.

Yes, always and everywhere, sin is an abusing of God. If sin could, sin would destroy God. If sin could, sin would pull God off His throne. Sin abuses God's authority — as that authority is interposed in God's law. Sin abuses God's justice — as if God would not punish. Sin abuses God's power — as if God could not act. Sin abuses God's wisdom — as if God's laws were not right and reasonable.

Sin abuses God's omniscience and knowledge — as if God did not see and observe. Sin abuses God's long-suffering, patience, and forbearance — as if God's Spirit would always strive with men.

Sin abuses God's warnings and threatenings — as if God were not to be feared. Sin abuses God's promises — as if God's promises were not to be regarded. Sin abuses God's hatred of sin, as if sin were not a direct contrariety to God's nature and will. Sin abuses the Lord's Christ — refusing and rejecting Him as to His person, His nature, His office — abusing Him as to His substitutionary death, His blood, His righteousness — showing forth a devilish neglect of the great Saviour and the great salvation.

Sin is an abuse of the Holy Spirit — a resisting, a quenching, a vexing of the Spirit. Sin is such an universal abuse of God, Father, Son, Holy Ghost, it is no wonder that they who see sin as did the Psalmist cry out with him:

> Against thee, thee only, have I sinned, and done this
> evil in thy sight: that thou mightest be justified when
> thou speakest, and be clear when thou judgest (Psalm
> 51:4).

Sin is an abuse of heaven. Sin built hell. And sin produces the worm that never dies. Sin kindled the fire that never shall be quenched (Mark 9:44) — where, environed by ghastly horrors, hell's infernal drums beat time to the ceaseless groans of the lost.

When sin so diabolically abuses the God of heaven, no wonder that it abuses man on earth and brings him into captivity. Sin is a malicious abuse of man's soul — so capable of glorious enjoyment in heaven. Because of sin, man's soul grovels in the dust — wallows in a filthy kennel.

Sin is a devilish abuse of man's body, which should be the temple of the Holy Ghost. Because of sin, man's body becomes the habitation of Satan — so that it is not found "always bearing about in the body the dying of the Lord Jesus that the life also of Jesus might be made manifest in the body" (II Corinthians 4:10).

Sin is a relentless abuse of time — that precious thing that should be used in bringing blessings to others, and in preparation for eternity. Sin is a wasteful abuse of health and strength — causing men to employ against God and the causes of Christ the health and strength God gives.

> Strangers have devoured his strength, and he knoweth it
> not: yea, gray hairs are here and there upon him, yet he
> knoweth not (Hosea 7:9).

Sin is a thieving abuse of riches and prosperity — causing people to forget that all we have comes from God. In this respect many are as guilty as was Jeshurun:

> But Jeshurun waxed fat, and kicked: thou art waxen fat,
> thou art grown thick, thou art covered with fatness; then
> he forsook God which made him, and lightly esteemed
> the Rock of his salvation (Deuteronomy 32:15).

Jeremiah describes men akin to Jeshurun: "How shall I pardon thee for this? thy children have forsaken me, and sworn by them that are no gods: when I had fed them to the full, they then committed adultery, and assembled themselves by troops in the harlots' houses" (Jeremiah 5:7). Sin causes men to give much of the money God has given them to their profane diversions, idle and vain and wanton amusements — their lewd and wicked practices. Sin is an abuse of warnings, afflictions, judgments, light, knowledge. How long it takes men to learn and to believe that men cannot sin at a cheap rate.

The heroine in Ibsen's dream urges her paramour to commit suicide, saying: "Do it beautifully." But an ugly thing like suicide can not be done "beautifully." Nor can one commit adultery "beautifully." Nor steal "beautifully."

Nothing that is not good is *really* beautiful — and everything else which seems so is only "what the degraded soul unworthily admires."

Sin is more than weakness — it is awful ugliness. In life it is the rattlesnake in the pansy bed — the death head set amidst life's feast, the desert breath that drinks up every dew.

The form of sin is often beautiful to the eye — and men long to embrace it. But when men clutch it, the lovely form always changes to a hideous skeleton that grins and chatters in man's face.

Moreover, sin is an abuse of God's Word — the written Word, the preached Word. It makes men wrest the Scriptures to their own destruction, causes men to impugn the necessity of divine revelation. That is one reason why today that we have scholastic clowns who summon the Bible to appear at the bar of human reason and a "Thus saith the mind of man" is substituted for a "Thus saith the Lord."

Sin is an abuse of wit, reason, talents, sermons, Sabbaths — everything men should value highly in this brief life on earth. And so, sin has made men captives.

Men are captives to the justice of God, to which we owe millions and millions, which cannot be paid until Christ redeems therefrom by satisfying all the demands of justice. Men are captives to the Law, as a covenant. The Law condemns us. All are condemned to the fire of hell by the Law — till Christ redeems us from the curse of the Law by being made a curse for us. For He was condemned in our room. Though innocent Himself He was imputatively guilty, when God laid on Him the iniquity of us all. Men are captives to their own consciences. That bosom-judge tells us we are enemies to God. It is a judge we cannot decline. It is a witness we cannot cast out. It is an executioner we can not resist. Men are, by nature, captives to Satan. He leads us captive at his pleasure. We by nature are his servants. We are the subjects — he is king. We are the shop where he works till Christ redeems us from this captivity — till the God-man binds the strong man and dispossesses him. Men are captives to divers lusts. One lust is hard enough to serve. But how hard to serve many. Not only variety but contrary ones — like so many wild horses drawing us contrary ways. The galley slave tugging at oar night and day is at perfect freedom compared to this. Redemption from this slavery is a great redemption.

Men, by sin, are captives to fear of death. Many are in great bondage all their days through fear. The prospect of the King of Terrors creates a horror in the soul — until Christ redeems from this by taking away both the sting of death and the terror of it. Our Lord Jesus redeems from these and from all the effects of sin. He redeems from the wrath of God, that omnipotent wrath, that irresistible wrath, that destructive wrath, that righteous wrath that none can stand before — one drop whereof would destroy thousands of angels.

Think now of the —

II. One Who Redeems

Jesus only is the Redeemer, "The stone which was set at nought of the builders, but which became the head of the corner" (Acts 4:11).

> Neither is there salvation in any other: for there is none other name under heaven given among men, whereby we must be saved (Acts 4:12).

We read these words: "Thou wast slain and hast redeemed us unto God by thy blood" (Revelation 5:9).

The Old Testament Redeemer is Jehovah God. We read: "For the Lord hath redeemed Jacob, and glorified himself in Israel" and "Thus saith the Lord, thy Redeemer" (Isaiah 41:23, 24).

> But now thus saith the Lord that created thee, O Jacob, and he that formed thee, O Israel, Fear not: for I have redeemed thee, I have called thee by thy name; thou art mine (Isaiah 43:1).
> Thus saith the Lord, thy Redeemer, the Holy One of Israel; I am the Lord thy God which teacheth thee to profit, which leadeth thee by the way that thou shouldest go (Isaiah 48:17).

Jeremiah, speaking of God and what He could do, said: "Their Redeemer is strong" (Jeremiah 50:34).

Indeed, as *Elohim* is the creative name, so *Jehovah* is the redemptive, covenant-keeping name of God.

God sent Jesus to redeem. He only frees from sin. He Himself says: "Verily, verily, I say unto you, He that heareth my word, and believeth on him that sent me, hath everlasting life, and shall not come into condemnation; but is passed from death unto life" (John 5:24).

Jesus only brings the quickening spirit. As by His Spirit He will raise up our natural body from death to life — so He raises our souls from the death of sin to the life of grace. "Who shall lay anything to the charge of God's elect? It is Christ who died" (Romans 8:33).

Sinful man's redemption was too transcendent a thing for any mere creation to be the redeemer of the sons of men. The children of Israel were afraid to trust an angel with their conduct into Canaan (Exodus 33). Much more should we be afraid to trust an angel or any other creature to make a way for our passage to the heavenly Canaan.

It was necessary that the Redeemer be a God-man.

> For such an high priest became us, who is holy, harmless, undefiled, separate from sinners, and made higher than the heavens (Hebrews 7:26).

He must, in God's redemptive purpose, lay down His life. This He could not have done had He not been a man. He took up His life again. This He could not have done if He had not been God. Thus we see that all contradictions meet in Jesus — our Redeemer.

Mystic is He, yet beautifully simple.

Earnest is He, yet never fierce.

Powerful is He, yet infinitely tender.

Humble is He, yet never cringing.

Dignified is He, yet never cold.

Human is He, yet divine — even deity.

The Redeemer is of God. "God so loved the world" (John 3:16).

Christ's substitution in our stead is of God. "The Lord hath laid on him the iniquity of us all" (Isaiah 53:6).

Christ's suffering in our stead is of God. "It pleased the Lord to bruise him" (Isaiah 53:10).

Christ's assuming our nature, that He might therein give Himself a sacrifice for our sins, is of *God* and of His sovereign will.

> Then said I, Lo, I come: in the volume of the book it is written of me, I delight to do thy will, O my God: yea, thy law is within my heart (Psalm 40:7, 8).

Christ's being made a curse and being made sin for us is of *God.*

> Christ hath redeemed us from the curse of the law, being made a curse for us: for it is written, Cursed is every one that hangeth on a tree (Galatians 3:13).
>
> For he hath made him to be sin for us, who knew no sin; that we might be made the righteousness of God in him (II Corinthians 5:21).

Christ's furniture and ability for His work of redemption is of *God.*

> Behold my servant, whom I uphold; mine elect, in whom my soul delighteth; I have put my spirit upon him: he shall bring forth judgment to the Gentiles (Isaiah 42:1).

Christ's resurrection and exaltation is of *God.* "Who by him do believe in God, that raised him up from the dead, and gave him glory; that your faith and hope might be in God" (I Peter 1:21).

In our redemption all is owning to God as the first cause.

Now we should note the —

III. MEANS OF OUR REDEMPTION

Great the life example Jesus gave us as He wore the white flower of a sinless life in the midst of a crooked and perverse generation — as He lived the life which was the very biography of perfume, the overflow of graciousness, the language of the unuttered, the thrill of the uncatalogued.

> For I have given you an example, that ye should do as I have done to you (John 13:15).

Great the teachings of Jesus — as in His teaching He gave revelation, not speculations; certainties, not surmises; guidance, not gropings; divine declarations, not human inquiries. "Never man spake like this man." And in His teachings Jesus leaped across conventional chasms, broke down artificial barriers, bridged chasms between sex and sex, sect and sect.

Great and marvelous the miracles of Jesus — from the human viewpoint. Jesus, a miracle greater than all His miracles, wrought miracles—making blind men to see, deaf men to hear, lepers to be clean, crazy men to have their minds restored, crippled men to walk, sick folks to be well, the dead to have life again.

But wherein lies the power of Jesus for redemption in all these things? In the amount of life He lived and gave? No. Jesus did not put enough redeeming life into what He did to save a single soul — aside from the sacrifice of Himself on Calvary where "he bore our sins in his own body on the tree" (I Peter 2:24).

Blood is taken for the whole suffering of Jesus — from the moment of His conception, from His miserable entry into this world in Bethlehem's barn in human flesh, until He breathed His last on the cross.

Life is in the blood. "For the life of the flesh is in the blood: and I have given it to you upon the altar to make an atonement for your souls: for it is the blood that maketh an atonement for the soul" (Leviticus 17:11).

Then, listen: "Thou wast slain and hast redeemed us unto God by thy blood" (Revelation 5:9).

Sinful man's redemption is by death and blood. This redemption is by death and blood. Jesus purchased redemption with His own blood in contrast with the silver and gold which were commonly used for human ransoms:

> Forasmuch as ye know that ye were not redeemed with corruptible things, as silver and gold, from your vain conversation received by tradition from your fathers; but with the precious blood of Christ, as of a lamb without blemish and without spot (I Peter 1:18, 19).
> In whom we have redemption through his blood, the forgiveness of sins, according to the riches of his grace (Ephesians 1:7).

Jesus, called "the Lamb slain from the foundation of the world," was slain secretively — by the determinate counsel and foreknowledge of God from all eternity. Jesus, who was slain typically under all the sacrifices by the Old Testament, whereby death was adumbrated and shadowed forth, was slain actually between two thieves upon Mount Calvary — where the sufferings of His life were consummated in the suffering of His death. He became obedient unto death, even the death of the cross, when He was wounded for our sins — our sins which were His murderers. The Jews and Romans were but executioners.

We do not say that a man who pulls the trigger on the gallows, who throws the switch in the death house, who turns on the gas in the lethal death chamber has the spirit of murder, or the like. But rather the man's theft and murder — they kill him.

So here it is not so much the Jews or soldiers who killed the Lord of Glory as our own sins — our sins, abominations and breaches of God's law, which sins were imputed to Him as surety, sins laid to His charge, who suffered, the Just for the unjust, that He might pay the debt we owed to divine justice. His body, in afflictions of the cross, and His soul, in agonies unspeakable, grappled with all the powers of heaven, earth and hell.

God has said: "Awake, O sword, against my shepherd, and against the man that is my fellow" (Zechariah 13:7). And the glittering sword of wrath and vengeance was thrust and sheathed into Christ's bowels with infinite terror and horror — making Christ's soul exceeding sorrowful, even unto death, and battering, buffeting, bruising, and breaking Him for our iniquities.

Once, over Jerusalem, He shed tears of water, but now, on the rack of justice, He shed tears of blood. "Thou wast slain, and hast redeemed us to God *by thy blood* . . ." (Revelation 5:9). Here is the price of redemption — the precious blood of the Son of God.

> Take heed therefore unto yourselves, and to all the flock, over the which the Holy Ghost hath made you overseers, to feed the church of God, which he hath purchased with his own blood (Acts 20:28).
>
> And almost all things are by the law purged with blood; and without shedding of blood is no remission (Hebrews 9:22).

In the Jewish thought, the life was in the blood, and the blood was the life. "Thou shalt not eat the flesh with the blood in it" ran the law, "for in the flesh is the blood, and the blood is the life."

Jesus Christ's atonement was a *blood* atonement.

> Then Jesus said unto them, Verily, verily, I say unto you,
> except ye eat the flesh of the Son of man, and drink his
> blood, ye have no life in you. Whoso eateth my flesh,
> and drinketh my blood, hath eternal life; and I will
> raise him up at the last day. For my flesh is meat indeed,
> and my blood is drink indeed. He that eateth my flesh,
> and drinketh my blood, dwelleth in me, and I in him.
> As the living Father hath sent me, and I live by the
> Father: so he that eateth me, even he shall live by me
> (John 6:53-57).

His death is mine — and appropriated by faith. Thus appropriated by faith, it becomes life in me. Thus we see that only in a *slain* Christ can poor sinners find that which meets their dire and solemn need. And His flesh He gave on the cross — in voluntary and vicarious and victorious sacrifice. His meritorious life was substituted for our forfeited life. Surely this will move our hearts to fervent praise. Eating His flesh and drinking His blood means simply this, beautifully this, only this: *We are to believe on Him as One who died for us and lives again as the Sustainer of our souls.* It is not a dead Christ the sinner is to feed upon, but the death of one who is alive forevermore. We are to appropriate His sacrifice and make it our own. The blood atones for your life in some strange way. The life of a beast was in its blood — and that life was made over to the credit of another. Animal sacrifices were made on the altars for this reason. When the animal was sacrificed on the altar the blood flowed out. The blood that flowed out carried the life with it — and the life went with the blood not staying in the beast.

To repeat, in Jewish thought, the blood was life. The body meant nothing. Blood meant everything. He who gave His blood, gave His life — and we are redeemed through the blood of Jesus Christ. The life blood must be poured from the veins. Christ poured out His life in the sacrifice on the cross before that life became available to you and to me. He put some of His life in His teachings. He put more of His life into His miracles. But the greatest was when with pierced and broken heart, He poured out the blood and with it the life. The crimson cord seen in the ceremonial and sacrificial offerings of the Old

Testament terminates in the blood-stained cross upon Calvary's hill. The slain doves and sheep were but signs pointing to the Lamb of God slain before the foundation of the world. All the sacrifices on the bloody altars were but shadows of redemptive entity still ahead, adumbrations of a substance yet to be, for Jesus bleeding unto death was the propellent center to which the faith of mankind before and since has gravitated.

The word "bless" comes from the Anglo-Saxon word for "blood." The interest of sinners was arrived at in the death of Christ. Redemption is buying back from under the power of some person or some thing. It is a purchase that results in the former controlling power being gone. In spiritual redemption, the soul is brought into a new position – a position of freedom from the penal consequences of sin. The soul in its unredeemed state is under the power of sin, the curse of the law, the influence of the present world, the frivolous habits of life, and the other spiritual enemies. The crimson coin of Christ's blood is the delivering power. The blood is the emancipating power. Its voice speaks liberty to the soul. And the Gospel is the authoritative proclamation which not only causes you to know that you are freed, but indicates to you how to bring out of sight and out of mind all memories of your past bondage.

And we thank God for the efficacy of Christ's blood. We read this as to the dedication of God's Temple in Jerusalem:

> And king Solomon offered a sacrifice of twenty and two thousand oxen, and an hundred and twenty thousand sheep (II Chronicles 7:5).

But the hymn writer, in acknowledgment of the cleansing power of Christ's blood, wrote:

> Not all the blood of beasts
>   On Jewish altars slain,
> Could give the guilty conscience peace,
>   Or wash away the stain.
> But Christ, the heavenly Lamb,
>   Takes all our sins away –
> A sacrifice of nobler name,
>   And richer blood than they.

Now give thought to –

IV. The Person to Whom Sinners Are Redeemed

"Thou hast redeemed us unto God" — as the first cause, as last end — to be God's sons, God's servants, God's friends, God's crown, God's glory. Yes, and to enjoy Him, to glorify Him, to be His peculiar treasure.

Christ died, "the Just One for the unjust that He might bring us to God" (I Peter 3:18). "For if, when we were enemies, we were reconciled to God by the death of his Son, much more, being reconciled, we shall be saved by his life" (Romans 5:10).

Redeemed to God!

Believers are redeemed to the *knowledge* of God.

> For God, who commanded the light to shine out of darkness, hath shined in our hearts, to give the light of the knowledge of the glory of God in the face of Jesus Christ (II Corinthians 4:6).

Man lost his view and knowledge of God by the fall. And no guilty sinner can know God, to his satisfaction, but in the red glass of the blood of Jesus, who hath redeemed us to God by His blood. We do not see God savingly until we see the Redeemer.

Believers are redeemed to the *favor* of God and to the *peace* of God. "And, having made peace through the blood of his cross, by him to reconcile all things unto himself; by him, I say, whether they be things in earth, or things in heaven" (Colossians 1:20).

Believers are redeemed to the *image* of God. "We are transformed into the same image from glory unto glory" (II Corinthians 3:18). "Who gave himself for us, that he might redeem us from all iniquity, and purifying unto himself a peculiar people, zealous of good works" (Titus 2:14). That He might bring us to God and to conformity to His image — by bringing us back to the *life* of God, to the *love* of God, to the *service* of God.

We are by nature alienated from the life of God. But He redeems from death to the life of God. He redeems from enmity to the love of God. He redeems from slavery to sin and Satan

to the service of God. He redeems from the state of stranger-
hood to the state of acquaintanceship.

Believers are redeemed to the *enjoyment* of God.

> And not only so, but we also joy in God through our
> Lord Jesus Christ, by whom we have now received the
> atonement (Romans 5:11).

Yes — to fellowship and communion with God, so as to have
possession of Him as our God — according to the covenant sealed
with the blood of Christ.

Somebody has called this the *introductory* enjoyment — trans-
lating Romans 5:2 in these words: "Through whom also, as the
result of faith, we have obtained an introduction." "But now in
Christ Jesus ye who sometimes were far off are made nigh by
the blood of Christ" (Ephesians 2:13).

What a contrast between these two states! From stranger-
hood to acquaintanceship. Before the sinner's introduction to
God in a friendly capacity, he is far from God. His heart is
in the world and his soul in his sins. There are no friendly rela-
tions between the sinner and God in the capacity of *Judge*. They
have never been introduced — and the sentence in all such cases
is: "Then will I profess unto them, I never knew you: depart
from me, ye that work iniquity" (Matthew 7:23).

Now the blood of Christ rectifies all this. It has the power
to bring us right into God's presence and introduce us to Him.
It is by the introductory power of the blood we obtain the
privilege of God's acceptance and have the right to stand before
Him. And it is on account of the blood that the King and Judge
of the whole world meets us in a friendly and forgiving spirit.
The *blood* is the badge of our admission. The introductory power
of the blood of Christ confers not only status but confident assurance. It provides us with an argument for whatever we
desire. The blood-bought soul has the right to come to God at
any time of the day or night and in any place and under any
circumstances and present his wants and wishes before the great
King — with the confident assurance that the whole earth will
reply to him. The blood removes every restriction — and it

entitles him to be well-received at the court of the King of heaven. Always and only through the blood can we dare to stand before God.

To us, some have spoken of this enjoyment of God as *consummative* enjoyment. The consummative enjoyment of him is in heaven. The enjoyment of him that is begun in the remission of sins and the regeneration of the fullness of the Godhead, that is in Christ, unto us, is at last consummated in the full and uninterrupted enjoyment of God in heaven — where communion with God is no more by faith but by vision — no more by hope, but by fruition. "For now we see through a glass, darkly; but then face to face: Now I know in part; but then shall I know even as also I am known" (I Corinthians 13:12).

To this consummated enjoyment of God we are redeemed by His blood — hence heaven is called the purchased possession. "Which is the earnest of our inheritance until the redemption of the purchased possession, unto the praise of his glory" (Ephesians 1:14).

And the heavenly singers make this the ecstatic theme of their redemptive song: "Thou wast *slain* and hast redeemed us *to God* by thy blood."

Thus believers are redeemed *to* — to the *knowledge* of God, to the *favour* of God, to the *image* of God, to the *enjoyment* of God — commenced and advanced graciously here, and consummated gloriously in God's heavenly Kingdom.

Thus by the blood of Christ, we are redeemed to God, to the kingdom of God, in grace and glory, and so to God as our chief good and last end — to have the Lord Jehovah to be our everlasting light and life and happiness, our exceeding great reward, our portion, our all in all.

Oh, this redemption through the blood of Christ is a redemption *of* God — as the first cause *and* a redemption *to* God, as the last end. Therefore, a redemption to be valued, as made of God to you for your everlasting happiness — and made of God to Himself for His everlasting glory. Therefore, as you would not trample on the blood of Christ, as you would regard your own everlasting happiness, which is a great matter, and God's everlasting glory which is greater — come, come to this blessed Redeemer and welcome a redemption made *of* God to redeem you *to* God, and to His highest honor and greatest glory. And I will tell you good news; *if* your heart welcome this great Redeemer in His bloody vesture — because He came from God to bring you to God, *if* you welcome this redemption — because it is made of God to redeem you unto God, *then* you may be assured that God welcomes you into His everlasting bosom, because His only begotten Son, who is in His bosom, is accepted as God's *Sent-One* to you. Therefore, says Christ: Verily, verily, I say unto you, He that heareth my word, and believeth on him that sent me, hath everlasting life, and shall not come into condemnation; but is passed from death unto life" (John 5:24).

So, I say, no duly elected member of the U. S. Senate has a better claim to a seat in the Senate than a blood-bought sinner has to a seat in the Father's house. His blood secures admission into heaven.

> And I said unto him, Sir, thou knowest. And he said to me, These are they which came out of great tribulation, and have washed their robes, and made them white in the blood of the Lamb (Revelation 7:14).

The washing in the blood of the Lamb is the explanation of their being there. Have you washed your soul in the blood of the Lamb? You say: "How can I do it?" How do you wash yourself? Why, you come with all your dirt and all your defilement to the fountain and you apply the water to your body with your own hand. In the same way do you wash in the blood of the Lamb in a *spiritual* sense. You take the blood and apply it to your soiled and guilty conscience with the hand of faith. You say, honestly: "Lord Jesus, I take you as my Saviour and your blood to cleanse me from my sins, and I rest and depend on thee henceforth."

Tell this to the Lord sincerely just wherever you are and whoever you are, honestly meaning it, and that will imply and make real washing in the blood of the Lamb.

Conquered Contraries

CHAPTER III

CONQUERED CONTRARIES

> And you, being dead in your sins and the uncircumcision of your flesh, hath he quickened together with him, having forgiven you all trespasses; blotting out the handwriting of ordinances that was against us, which was contrary to us, and took it out of the way, nailing it to his cross (Colossians 2:13, 14).

The cross of Christ was a goal in the heart of God from all eternity. It was part of the everlasting purpose of God, not just a device which God used to extricate Himself from the dilemma in which He unexpectedly found Himself after Adam, the federal head of the race, plunged into sin. All scenes of blood and blackness which had the cross for a center — all the scars Jesus received when He was bruised and battered for our iniquities — God had seen in that dateless eternity when His love for men had devised the means by which, after man's fall in Adam, God would bring sinful men back to Himself.

In those eternal ages it was the glory of the cross which filled the heart of God, the Father — of God, the Son — of God, the Holy Spirit. When Christ, the Creator, was born of the creature woman, was made flesh; when He came down from the heights of deity to the depths of humanity, the terrors, the shame and anguish of the cross pressed upon Him with the weight of worlds. "A Lamb as it had been slain" is the vision of the coming eternity. The cross was the place of torture, of tragedy, of taunts, of triumph. It was triumph because, though Jesus Himself was nailed to the cross, He nailed all that was contrary to us to that same cross — His cross. And how much there was against us all the Scriptures testify:

53

> All my bones shall say, Lord, who is like unto thee, which
> deliverest the poor from him that is too strong for him,
> yea, the poor and the needy from him that spoileth him?
> (Psalm 35:10).

Thus do His members praise Christ, "in whom we have redemption through his blood, even the forgiveness of sins" (Colossians 1:14). Thus do His members praise Him who is "head over
all things to the church" (Ephesians 1:22) — "the head of the
body, the church" (Colossians 1:18). Thus do the members
praise their glorious Head — always and everywhere all powerful for their deliverance.

But let us ask, what was contrary to us? What were the
things He nailed to the cross — things contrary to us?

Against us, contrary to us, was —

I. THE CURSE OF THE LAW

> For as many as are of the works of the law are under
> the curse: for it is written, cursed is every one that con-
> tinueth not in all things which are written in the book of
> the law to do them (Galatians 3:10).

Therefore, we learn that the Law was too strong for the poor,
too strong for the needy, too strong for the rich, too strong for
the wise, too strong for the mighty, too strong for all. Consequently, no man can, by the Law, be justified in the sight of
the holy God because no man ever lived who never sinned. "All
have sinned." And you can find hogs with feathers and geese
which use fins for wings as easily as you can find a man who ever
lived who did not sin — except Jesus who "wore the white
flower of a blameless life in the midst of a crooked and perverse
generation."

Adam and Eve sinned, by sin were woefully deranged. And
grievous was their sin, dismantling the human race of its
nobility. Abraham, in whom the graces of the Hebrew race
were summarized, sinned, lying by saying that his wife, Sarai,
was his sister instead of his wife. Noah, a man who walked with
God in his generation (Genesis 6:9), "planted a vineyard, drank
of the wine and was drunken" (Genesis 9:20, 21). Moses, refusing to be called the son of Pharaoh's daughter, choosing
rather to suffer affliction with the people of God, esteeming the

reproach of Christ greater riches than the treasures in Egypt, forsaking Egypt, not fearing the wrath of the king, as seeing Him who is invisible (Hebrews 11), sinned. He killed an Egyptian, whom he found smiting a Hebrew, and hid him in the sand. Joseph, though he refused the dirty proposal of Potiphar's wife, though he took famine fear from the heart of a nation, was doubtless guilty of a sinful pride as he thought of his dreams when he beheld the sun and the moon and the eleven stars making obeisance to him (Genesis 37:9). Jacob, though God spake to him and blessed him beyond all deserving, dealt in crookedness and was guilty of despicable trickery.

Elijah, "God's whirlwind whelped by the desert," God's prophet of fire who called an apostate nation back to God, sinned. He was caught in the grip of despair and prayed to God to let him die before God's appointed time. Jonah, behind the curtain of whose preaching old Nineveh shifted scenes of riot for penitential tears, played the coward by going a different direction from the direction God pointed out and by sulking poutingly at the manifestation of God's mercy.

David sinned grievously, being guilty of adultery and murder. John the Baptist, who descended upon the iniquities of his day with a torch in one hand and a sword in the other, sinned. He doubted Jesus, sending a committee to Jesus, asking: "Art thou he that should come or look we for another?" Isaiah, in whose preaching were the thunder and lightning of Sinai and the foregleams of Calvary, "in the year when King Uzziah died," seeing God in a vision, confessed his sin, saying: "Woe is me, for I am undone — because I am a man of unclean lips" (Isaiah 6:5). Job, though he maintained his faith in God against great odds, confessed that his comeliness had turned into corruption. Peter, though he followed Christ to crucifixion, looked back upon the time when he forsook Jesus, denying Him, emphasizing his denial by vociferous cursing. John, though later he was called the apostle of love, wanted to call down fire from heaven upon a village. Paul, though later he stormed the capitals of proud empires in the name of Jesus, never forgot that he persecuted Christians — men and women and children — unto death.

All these and many others whom we could mention who did many mighty works under the hand of God, were targets of Satan and did not always escape the arrows from Satan's quiver and bow. The mark of sin is upon them and their records, even as such is upon us today.

> If we say that we have no sin, we deceive ourselves, and the truth is not in us. If we confess our sins, he is faithful and just to forgive us, and to cleanse us from all unrighteousness. If we say that we have not sinned, we make him a liar, and his word is not in us (I John 1:8-10).

No man can be justified by the Law in the sight of God. But Christ has redeemed His people from the curse of the Law, for He took the curse upon Himself when He hung on the tree. He nailed it to the cross — taking it out of the way — opening up to all believers in His finished work the road to God and glory.

> For by grace are ye saved through faith; and that not of yourselves: it is the gift of God (Ephesians 2:8).
> For as many as are of the works of the law are under the curse: for it is written, Cursed is every one that continueth not in all things which are written in the book of the law to do them . . . . Christ hath redeemed us from the curse of the law, being made a curse for us: for it is written, Cursed is every one that hangeth on a tree (Galatians 3:10, 13).

We pitch our mental tents on this verse, we gather our hearts' meditations about this statement, as those who approach a holy white sanctuary where unanointed feet can not walk! *"Made a curse for us!"*

Jesus, so finely strung, so unutterably keyed to truth, mercy, justice, love, quickly feeling the sorrow, sympathy and indignation which injustice and wrong invariably elicit from all high souls — "made a curse." Jesus, Inhabitor of Eternity — "made a curse"; Jesus, Teacher come from God — "made a curse"! Jesus, image of the invisible God, the first born of every creature" — "made a curse"!

Jesus, "Light of light," hanging in darkness when "the sun went down at noonday and the earth was darkened in the clear day" — "made a curse"!

Jesus, "Poet's Poet, Wisdom's Tongue, Man's Best Man, good Paragon, Crystal Christ" — "made a curse"! Jesus, "the brightness of God's glory and the express image of his person" — "made a curse"! Jesus, "who had glory with the Father before the world was," "giving his back to the smiters and His cheeks to them who plucked off His beard, and hiding not His face from shame and spitting" — "made a curse"!

Jesus, "the Father's comprehensibility and visibility" — "made a curse." Jesus, "heir of all things," "Fairer than all the fair who fill the heavenly train" — "made a curse"! He who was earth's greatest blessing was "made a curse"!

Never was Christ a curse to anybody. He was "made a curse" *for* everybody. The curse due us fell crushingly on Him, for God laid on Him the iniquity of us all.

Deuteronomy records the penalty of the curse. It reads: "His body shall not remain on a tree, but thou shalt in any wise bury him that day (for he that is hanged is accursed of God) that thy land be not defiled, which the Lord thy God giveth thee for an inheritance" (Deuteronomy 21:23).

Thus do we read and thus do we understand that the curse of the *Law*, contrary to all, remaineth upon those who seek to justify themselves.

Jesus Christ, in whom all beauty, holiness, perfection, meet, possessing manhood in its purity and Godhead in its vastness, tears of sympathy for our woes and eyes of fire to wither iniquity, Son of Abraham, Son of David, Son of Man, Son of God, the personal, voluntary, self-emptying Redeemer, exhausts the precious treasures of His invaluable blood to pay our debts. He only is the everlasting source of human salvation. He only, by a work consistent with the character of God, can break the power which holds us in chains, avert the punishment which threatens us, fortify with fresh sanctions the law which we had broken, and reconciling justice with mercy, open to mankind the fountains of grace. Through Him the law is vindicated, the holiness of God doubly honored, and mercy in richest munificence proclaimed to the sinner — so that the sinner, by faith in Jesus, is enabled to give his testimony:

> Out of my bondage, sorrow and night,
> Jesus, I come; Jesus, I come;
> Into Thy freedom, gladness and light,
> Jesus, I come to Thee.
> Out of my sickness into Thy health,
> Out of my want and into Thy wealth,
> Out of my sin and into Thyself,
> Jesus, I come to Thee.

Against us, contrary to our welfare, is —

II. Sin

Sin is so devilishly contrary to us and to all that is for the welfare of mankind — in life and in death, in time and in eternity. Sin, reversing the harmony of man's being, undermining the constitutional order of man's nature, dismantling man of his nobility, bringing him in unconditional surrender to diabolical power, bringing the curse upon man, was what Christ nailed to His cross. Sin, so diabolically contrary to man's soul, Jesus nailed to His cross.

> For what the law could not do, in that it was weak through the flesh, God sending His own Son in the likeness of sinful flesh, and for sin, condemned sin in the flesh (Romans 8:3).
> For he hath made him to be sin for us, who knew no sin; that we might be made the righteousness of God in him (II Corinthians 5:21).

Our past has been one of missing the mark, of going astray, of walking in evil ways, of falling short of God's glory, of possessing hearts "deceitful above all things and desperately wicked." Our past has been one of foolish failure, of iniquitous inperfection, of dishonorable defeat. Our past has been one of levity in lawlessness, of stubbornness in rebellion, of enormity in enmity. Our past has been one of ugly ungodliness, of hellish hostility, of degrading defilement. Our past has been one of guilt, of condemnation, of sin, of the works of the flesh. And this sinful past that haunts us as Banquo's ghost must be dealt with before we can have access to God or acceptance with God.

In His death upon His cross, Christ took sin's place, took our place, took every man's place as God dealt with Jesus as He must deal with sin — in severe and unrelenting judgment. In His death upon the cross, Christ paid my debt, bore my punishment, put away my sin. And all He did avails for my salvation and redemption the moment I, by faith, accept Him as Saviour.

The Word of God declares: "The soul that sinneth it shall die." The Word of God declares: "There is not a just man in the earth that doeth good and sinneth not." The Word of God declares: "The wages of sin is death." The Word of God declares: "After death, the judgment."

Looking back upon the past every person born of woman, save the sinless Christ, must say what Pharaoh said, "I have sinned." What Achan said, "I have sinned." What King Saul said, "I have sinned." What King David said, "I have sinned." What the wandering son said, "I have sinned." That is what all of us must say as we fasten eyes of scrutiny and observation upon the past.

And our past must be dealt with. Resolving to do better now, to live righteously now, will not undo the sin of the past. Resolving now to throw down every idol and to cast out every foe will not answer for the sin we committed yesterday. Resolutions to hew to pieces now some spared Agag of worldliness will not suffice to deal with the past. Reformation now does not go deep enough. There must be remission. There must be redemption. There must be regeneration. Our past, as we know, as all men know, as God knows, is one of sin. And sin, an opiate in the will, a madness in the brain, a poison in the heart, a midnight blackness that invests man's whole moral being, the intolerable burden of a soul destined to live forever, is against God.

In words not altogether mine, I declare this stark and startling truth:

Sin is darkness — and it must be lighted.
Sin is degradation — and it must be removed.
Sin is disease — and it must be healed.
Sin is defilement — and it must be cleaned.

Sin is death — and it must be abolished.

Sin is debt — and it must be paid.

Sin is dross — and it must be burned out.

There is only one way for God to banish the darkness of sin, to remove the degradation of sin, to heal the disease of sin, to cleanse the defilement of sin, to abolish the death of sin, to pay the debt of sin, and at the same time be consistent with His holiness. The way is for Him to collect payment in full for our sin. And that is by judgment and death. This He has done in the redeeming work of our blessed Lord and Saviour.

Jesus Christ! He paid the debt. He died the death. He cleanses from the defilement. He heals the disease. He removes the degradation. He is the Light. If we acknowledge our bankruptcy to Christ, we find that He pays the debt. He removes the stain. He gives us an acceptable standing before God.

> For the law of the Spirit of life in Christ Jesus hath made me free from the law of sin and death (Romans 8:2).
>> Day and night, our Jesus makes no pause,
>> Pleads His own fulfillment of all laws,
>> Veils with His perfectness mortal flaws,
>> Clears the culprit, pleads the desperate cause,
>> Plucks the dead from Death's devouring paws,
>> And the worm that gnaws.
>> The blood that purchased our release
>> And purged our crimson stains,
>> We challenge earth and Hell to show
>> A sin it can not cleanse.

Another thing so contrary to us, which thing Jesus hath taken out of the way, nailing it to His cross, is —

III. The World

In thinking of "the world" we must remember that the Christian who seeks to do the will of God everywhere and all the time can no more escape opposition from the contrary world than a swimmer in the river can escape dampness, no more than one can stick his hand in the fire and escape burning. The Christian and the world are, as Dr. Riley expresses it, constitutionally opposed — in life, in customs, in influence. By this we do not hold the erroneous idea that matter is inherently evil — because "the world," according to the Biblical use, does not refer to the globe we inhabit, but rather to man in his fallen state, to mankind in universal degeneracy.

Now the Christian must live in the world — just as a ship to make a voyage must be in the water; but, as Paul says, he must be "not conformed" to it — even as the ocean must not be in the voyaging ship — or the ship at anchor — because, in this life, the world, ever from below, and the Christian, born from above, are necessarily enemies. Paul knew that from experience when he wrote:

> For the good that I would I do not: but the evil which I would not, that I do. Now if I do that I would not, it is no more I that do it, but sin that dwelleth in me. I find then a law, that, when I would do good, evil is present with me. For I delight in the law of God after the inward man. But I see another law in my members, warring against the law of my mind, and bringing me into captivity to the law of sin which is in my members (Romans 7:19-23).

The world — portrayed in these phrases, "the lust of the flesh," "the lust of the eyes," "the pride of life" — stands for that sphere of evil, for the spirit among mankind that is in direct hostility to Christ and Christ's teachings. The world, under the sway of some power essentially hostile to God, is a world living in darkness, rejecting the light. It is a world under condemnation, needing heaven's mercy, yet refusing the spirit of truth.

The Christian is warned to "love not the world." "Love not the world, neither the things that are in the world. If any man love the world, the love of the Father is not in him" (I John 2:15).

"Friendship of the world is enmity with God" (James 4:4). Is the world, wholly evil, to be fought, and to be conquered? Jesus answers: "I have overcome the world" (John 16:33). John says: "Whosoever is born of God overcometh the world" (I John 5:4). Paul, knowing of the world enemy within our world, said:

> But God forbid that I should glory, save in the cross of our Lord Jesus Christ, by whom the world is crucified unto me, and I unto the world (Galatians 6:14).

To the individual that "world" to whom this great preacher was crucified is "the inordinate love of the things of this world of evil" — its riches, its power, its pleasures, the things that cause men to be filled with the world's spirit.

The world, therefore, is contrary to us — cheating us if we go the direction it points and follow the road it devises.

> Love not the world, neither the things that are in the world. If any man love the world, the love of the Father is not in him. For all that is in the world, the lust of the flesh, and the lust of the eyes, and the pride of life, is not of the Father, but is of the world (I John 2:15-17).

And the world passeth away, and the lust thereof: but he that doeth the will of God abideth forever.

The world is too much with us. The world promises substance and then cheats with the shadow. The world promises velvet and then gives a shroud. The world promises liberty and then gives slavery. The world promises nectar and then gives gall. The world promises good fruit and then gives rinds and hulls. The world promises perfumed garments and then gives rotten rags. The world promises silk and then gives sackcloth. The world promises coronations and then gives mimic crowns, ghostly garlands. The world promises bright revelry and then provides burlesque in the end. The world promises splendors and then gives faded spangles. The world promises sleep and then gives nightmares. The world promises heat and warmth and then gives painted fire. The world promises bread and then gives photographic bread. The world promises rest and gives weariness. The world is impotent to give what we need most in life and death, in youth and old age, in Time and Eternity as is an infant's arm to chain the lightning, as is a toothpick to tunnel a mountain, as is a teaspoon in an invalid's hand to stay the mad plunge of an avalanche, as is a toy hammer in a baby's hand to pound the pyramids of Egypt to dust, as is a circus clown to set marching again the army of Xerxes.

The world is a burglar of Life's treasure chest. The world is a wrecker on Life's railroad. The world poisons Life's cup. The world's pillows are filled with thorns. The world's practice is a bread of deceit — at first sweet, but afterwards the mouth is filled with gravel. The world is a bandit. The world gives no refuge in trouble. The world gives no comfort in sorrow. The world gives no courage in disaster. The world gives no judgment in clamor. The world gives no light in darkness. The world gives no calm in storms. The world is the coral reef on which hope's ships are wrecked.

The world, "too much with us," as Wordsworth says, is a Joab — greeting us with brotherly words and putting the sword under the fifth rib:

> When they were at the great stone which is in Gideon, Amasa went before them. And Joab's garment that he had put on was girded unto him, and upon it a girdle with a sword fastened upon his loins in the sheath thereof; and as he went forth it fell out. And Joab said to Amasa, Art thou in health, my brother? And Joab took Amasa by the beard with the right hand to kiss him. But Amasa took no heed to the sword that was in Joab's hand: so he smote him therewith in the fifth rib, and shed out his bowels to the ground (II Samuel 20:8-10).

The world is a treacherous Absalom — doing us obeisance, putting forth a friendly hand, subtly striving to steal our hearts from love and loyalty to God, yet seeking the while to drive us from our God-given throne. "Absalom stole the hearts of the people" and "Absalom reigned in Hebron" and "the people increased continually with Absalom" — and "the King went forth . . . . and tarried in a place that was far off" (II Samuel 15).

The world is a seductive Delilah — enticing us — seeing by what means it may prevail against us that it may blind us and it may bind us and afflict us, vexing our souls unto death — even as Delilah got Samson's strength (Judges 16).

The world is in pretense a hospitable host — a Jael — giving us milk when we ask water only, bringing forth butter in a lordly dish, yet putting the hand to the nail and the workman's hammer and striking us through the temples and nailing our heads to the earth — rejoicing in our deaths (Judges 5).

The world is an evil, left-handed Ehud, hiding its dagger under its gaudy raiment, offering us gifts in the fatness of our prosperity, and then, claiming that it has for us a message from God, thrusting its deadly dagger into us even as we stretch forth our hand in friendly and fraternal greeting (Judges 3).

The world is a treacherous Judas, professing love with kisses and soft words, yet eager to betray us unto death, working ever on the side of the foes of our soul.

Yes, the world is a vulture in peacock's feathers, a wolf in sheep's clothing, a tarantula spitting venom, not honey, into life's cup — promising pleasure and giving pain, promising health and giving sickness, promising us rest and spreading a couch of thorns and giving pillows filled with thistles. Yes, the world, having both wealth and poverty, one bloated, the other lean, is "too much with us." The world, having its Dives vivid with apoplexy and its Lazarus pale with anemia, is loved too much and by too many. Yes, the world, ever bruising us and never blessing us, is, as Hume said, "a fleeting show."

The world, ever a mirage to the thirsty, painted and distant fire for the cold, photographed bread for the hungry, will hate us if we announce our faith in, our allegiance to, and show determination to follow Christ.

> If the world hate you, ye know that it hated me before it hated you. If you were of the world, the world would love his own: but because ye are not of the world, but I have chosen you out of the world, therefore the world hateth you (John 15:18, 19).

The man who lives in enmity with God because he is a friend of the world is as the man who is partner with the thief, hating his own soul, as a man forced to weave his own shroud and dig his own grave, as a man who feedeth his soul on corn or the wind, never being fed. We must conquer the world, overcome the world, which Christ overcame, nailing it to His cross.

The world is passing. "The world passeth away." Love not that which is passing, possessing no permanence. "The end of the world" is not a poetic or philosophical phrase; it is a Biblical sentence. What folly for the Christian, immortalized by his conversion, to fix his affections upon and give his talents to that which passeth away. But, as born-again people, we can over-

come the world, through Christ conquer the world, so contrary
to us:

> For whatsoever is born of God overcometh the world; and
> this is the victory that overcometh the world, even our
> faith. Who is he that overcometh the world, but he that
> believeth that Jesus is the Son of God? (I John 5:4, 5).

Yet another reality, so dastardly and deceitfully contrary to
us, is —

IV. THE FLESH

Without condemning these bodies of ours, the Scripture says:
"Mortify the body." Man, who is not his body, but who has a
body, has to do with the body, the flesh. Paul speaks of living
in the flesh.

> I am crucified with Christ: nevertheless I live; yet not I,
> but Christ liveth in me: and the life which I now live in
> the flesh I live by the faith of the Son of God, who loved
> me, and gave himself for me (Galatians 2:20).

Peter speaks of the flesh being contrary to us:

> Forasmuch then as Christ hath suffered for us in the flesh,
> arm yourselves likewise with the same mind: for he that
> hath suffered in the flesh hath ceased from sin; that he
> no longer should live the rest of his time in the flesh to
> the lusts of men, but to the will of God (I Peter 4:1, 2).

The strongest of the strong is this "contrary" old nature. We
need to take heed and be warned by these words:

> For the flesh lusteth against the Spirit, and the Spirit
> against the flesh: and these are contrary the one to the
> other: so that ye can not do the things that ye would.
> But if ye be led of the Spirit, ye are not under the law.
> Now the works of the flesh are manifest, which are
> these: adultery, fornication, uncleanness, lasciviousness,
> idolatry, witchcraft, hatred, variance, emulations, wrath,
> strife, seditions, heresies, envyings, murders, drunkenness,
> revellings, and such like: of which I tell you before, as I
> have also told you in time past, that they which do such
> things shall not inherit the kingdom of God (Galatians
> 5:14-21).
> And they that are Christ's have crucified the flesh with
> the affections and lusts (Galatians 5:24).

Because, in this froth-wave age, multitudes over-emphasize
"the flesh," we should give heed to the words: "This I say then,
Walk in the Spirit, and ye shall not fulfill the lust of the flesh"
(Galatians 5:16).

We live in a day when over-emphasis of the flesh is one of our current idolatries — when many "expose femininity for price and patronage." The prominence of the flesh stampedes us to-day — with vulgar dances named after animals, with suggestive pictures, with bathing beauty shows, with fashions that make their "sex appeal," showing as much of a woman's person as possible. On the stage, before which millions gather, there are bedroom and bathroom scenes — giving "the flesh . . ." highest seat in the spotlight. In magazines social problems, with the sex matter prominent, are discussed — all the froth and the meat (if perchance there be any meat) spiced with pepper from the devil's pepper pot. Many articles in the women's section of smart magazines advise "the female of the species" to catch the eyes of males with a flaming red hat, fascinate them with clothes that "make a woman look gorgeously curvaceous." And, as many have said, as we all know, as nearly all news stands show, there are some magazines and some newspapers that seem to rejoice in nudity and nastiness, their headlines and illustrations being heavily and gaudily soaked in sex. In a day when the chiefest of all appetites is the sex appetite, it seems we are, as Dr. Purvis says it, so naively delighted in having dis-covered that the Eternal made us male and female that we some-times seem to be forgetting that He made us anything else.

In our days of steam-heated, well-lighted houses, and dimly-lighted houses that militate against home life, of cunningly up-holstered furniture, human ingenuity exhausts every resource to provide new comforts for "the flesh." "Soothingly immersed in comforts," many worship their bodies — sublimate them, feed them, poison them with booze, pillow them in luxury — for-getting what Carlyle wrote:

> Seated within this body's car,
> The silent self is driven far.
> And the five senses at the pole,
> Like steeds are tugging — restive of control.
> And if the driver lose his way
> And see not aright — who can say
> Into what blind paths, what pits of fear
> Will plunge these chargers in their mad career?

Forgetting, too, that saintliness and crucifixion of the body are synonymous we heed not the truth that we should be —

> Always bearing about in the body the dying of the Lord Jesus, that the life also of Jesus might be made manifest in our body. For we which live are always delivered unto death for Jesus' sake, that the life also of Jesus might be made manifest in our mortal flesh (II Corinthians 4:10, 11).

Many, forgetting, if they ever knew it, the truth that the New Testament teaches that many dangers come to the immortal soul through gratification of the mortal body, let sin reign in the mortal body — obeying it in the lusts thereof.

Many strong men and many beautiful women, recognizing not the danger of fleshly ascendancy, yield not their bodies and the members thereof as instruments of righteousness unto God.

Many, remembering not that the body is not for fornication but for the Lord, keep not their bodies under, as Paul said he did — glorifying not God in their bodies, as every one grateful for God's mercies and for Christ's death on the cross should do.

This poem, bearing the stamp of age, yet youthful with wisdom for us today, we can ponder — holding the warning and holding the wisdom therein found:

> Three ghosts met upon a lonesome road,
> And spake each to one another,
> "How came that dark stain upon your mouth?
>   Brother, my brother?"
> "From eating of forbidden fruit,
>   Brother, my brother."
>
> Three ghosts met upon a winding road,
> And spake each to one another,
> "How came that burn upon your foot,
> No dust or ash may cover?"
> "I stamped a neighbor's heart-flame out,
>   Brother, my brother."
>
> Three ghosts met upon a darkened road
> And spake each to one another,
> "How came that blood upon your hand
> No silken glove may cover?"
> "From breaking of a woman's heart,
>   Brother, my brother."

> Three ghosts met upon a muddy road;
> The glutton, the thief, the lover,
> And sought their evil deeds to cover,
> But naked the soul goes up to God,
>   Brother, my brother.

But, though you forget much that I have written, hold fast the truth that we can, through Christ, be more effective in conquering the flesh, that mysterious thing so contrary to us, than are a ton of sod and a lake of water in cleansing, when used for that purpose, a single human body. Remember, too, that he who seeks not the help of Christ in conquering the flesh, in keeping the body under, is as a city with open gates and broken-down walls when besieged by cruel enemies. "If ye live after the flesh, ye shall die" (Romans 8:13). We should remember here, moreover, that he who for a while is victor over the flesh and then becomes victim of the flesh presents no prettier sight than a dog returning to his vomit or a sow to her wallowing in the mire.

But still another reality contrary to us is —

V. The Devil

The Apostle John spoke of him when he wrote:

> I have written unto you, fathers, because ye have known him that is from the beginning. I have written unto you, young men, because ye are strong, and the word of God abideth in you, and ye have overcome the wicked one (I John 2:14).

That wicked one is our arch-enemy — a deceiver of all men, striving to destroy all whom he can. Though there are those — some in ignorance, some basking conceitedly in the light of academic lustre — who belittle the devil and deny his existence and try to explain him into the vacancy of nothingness, still the fact of the arch-enemy Satan, the evil one, is a fact as certain as any fact of history is credible.

Though we may argue much and often, Satan, the old devil, is the personal tempter of men and the enemy of God — the mighty despiser of all that God approved. And Satan himself uses a master stroke in his own behalf when he gets people to deny that he is — no matter what the Bible and Christ and the experience of all centuries of human history may be.

But most clearly is the personality of the devil taught in the Bible. Fifteen of the books of the blessed Bible mention him no less than one hundred and seventeen times. And in each case he is spoken of as a real being. Just here I love to think of what Dr. Purvis wrote: "If there is no personal devil, the Master was either deceived or deceiving. I would not like to think of Him as either, for in no case did Jesus seem to lack intelligence, or be ignorant of mental, moral, or spiritual things. The Bible conceives of the devil, not as the original or only source of evil, but as its supreme personal representative. A personal devil is more understandable than a mere abstraction."

But do not think that the serpent of Genesis was just a snake. That serpent was Satan himself — Satan who "passes one hundred gates and finds one unlatched," as a strategist who knows every trick of warfare and who, pretending defeat and then leading into ambush, catching us going and coming, attacking us when our desire is strongest and our resistance weakest. As Meyer points out, the serpent is found in the third chapter from the beginning of the Bible and in the third chapter from the end of the Bible. We have "that old serpent, the Devil."

"And he laid hold on the dragon, that old serpent, which is the Devil, and Satan, and bound him a thousand years" (Revelation 20:2).

As men wiser than I have said, so say I, that the picture found in some children's "Story of the Bible" as a snake wound around the limb of a tree with his head hanging down to whisper into the ear of Eve is not from the Word of God. We believe he appeared to Eve just exactly as indicated in these words:

> But I fear, lest by any means, as the serpent beguiled Eve through his subtilty, so your minds should be corrupted from the simplicity that is in Christ (II Corinthians 11:3).
> And no marvel; for Satan himself is transformed into an angel of light (II Corinthians 11:14).

With Meyer, with others who believe God's Bible, I believe that he dazzled her by the brilliance of his appearance because he is presented in Scripture as one of the most beautiful beings, one of the most wonderful, most intellectual and musical beings ever created.

> Son of man, take up a lamentation upon the king of Tyrus, and say unto him, Thus saith the Lord God; Thou sealest up the sum, full of wisdom, and perfect in beauty. Thou hast been in Eden the garden of God; every precious stone was thy covering, the sardius, topaz, and the diamond, the beryl, the onyx, and the jasper, the sapphire, the emerald, and the carbuncle, and gold: the workmanship of thy tabrets and of thy pipes was prepared in thee in the day that thou wast created. Thou art the anointed cherub that covereth; and I have set thee so: thou wast upon the holy mountain of God; thou hast walked up and down in the midst of the stones of fire. Thou wast perfect in thy ways from the day that thou wast created, till iniquity was found in thee. By the multitude of thy merchandise they have filled the midst of thee with violence, and thou hast sinned: therefore I will cast thee as profane out of the mountain of God: and I will destroy thee, O covering cherub, from the midst of the stones of fire. Thine heart was lifted up because of thy beauty, thou hast corrupted thy wisdom by reason of thy brightness: I will cast thee to the ground, I will lay thee before kings, that they may behold thee. Thou hast defiled thy sanctuaries by the multitude of thine iniquities, by the iniquity of thy traffick; therefore will I bring forth a fire from the midst of thee, it shall devour thee, and I will bring thee to ashes upon the earth in the sight of all them that behold thee. All they that know thee among the people shall be astonished at thee: thou shalt be a terror, and never shall thou be any more. Again the word of the Lord came unto me, saying, Son of man, set thy face against Zidon, and prophesy against it (Ezekiel 28: 12-21).

Here we learn that he was full of wisdom — possessed of a full measure of creature wisdom.

Commenting on this, Meyer says: "We believe that he is the highest of all created beings, that in all probability he stood next to the Son of God Himself in glory. His original condition was one of perfection. His original name was Lucifer, which means 'light bearer' or 'bright and shining one.'"

Satan was perfect in beauty — in creature beauty. The Bible tells us he has *power*. The Bible tells us he has beauty. The

Bible tells us he has musical ability. The Bible tells us he has wrath. The Bible tells us he has wiles. The Bible tells us he has snares. The Bible tells us he has ministers. The Bible tells us he has angels.

Thus we see that he does much evil. When a man is tempted by the drink habit and becomes the victim of booze — that is Satan. Some are tempted and enter into sin like a fly who enters the spider's parlor. That is Satan. Some are enticed by the scarlet woman with her much fair speech, going after her as an ox to the slaughter, or as a fool to the correction of the stocks, seeming not to know that "her house is the way to hell, going down to the chambers of death." That is Satan.

Whatever else you do, whatever else you fail to do, "overcome the wicked one" — because he is crafty beyond human thought. Remember, as we have been advised, that your position is that of the duelist and that you must overcome this wicked one who is eternal in his vigilance and "cruel beyond human imagination" or be overcome. To be overcome by him is "the defeat of manhood, the overthrow of nobility, the loss of God Himself." As. Dr. Riley says: "To lose this battle against the devil is to lose life; to gain it is to gain life — to get the victory of victories, the crown of crowns."

Without Christ we will lose this battle against the devil. Through Christ, we can overcome the devil as Abraham conquered King Chedorlaomer, as Moses overcame Pharaoh, as Joshua overcame the five kings. Read of Joshua's conquest:

> Then said Joshua, Open the mouth of the cave, and bring out those five kings unto me out of the cave. And they did so, and brought forth those five kings unto him out of the cave, the king of Jerusalem, the king of Hebron, the king of Jarmuth, the king of Lachish, and the king of Eglon. And it came to pass, when they brought out those kings unto Joshua, that Joshua called for all the men of Israel, and said unto the captains of the men of war which went with him, Come near, put your feet upon the necks of these kings. And they came near, and put their feet upon the necks of them. And Joshua said unto them, Fear not, nor be dismayed, be strong and of good courage: for thus shall the Lord do to all your enemies

against whom ye fight. And afterward Joshua smote them, and slew them, and hanged them on five trees: and they were hanging upon the trees until the evening (Joshua 10:22-26).

Christ for us overcomes the devil even as David slew Goliath in behalf of Saul's army, even as Elijah overcame the prophets of Baal in the days of Israel's apostasy, even as Ebed-melech overcame people in the rescue of Jeremiah from the dungeon, even as Samson carried off the gates of Gaza, even as Elisha overcame the enemy army at Dothan.

The devil is mighty but he is not *almighty* as is Jesus. The cross was the devil's bitterest foe. "They overcame him, that is the *devil*, by the blood of the Lamb." Through His death, Jesus made the power of the devil to be of none effect, to be as futile as a fence made of macaroni straws to stop the stampede of wild cattle. Whatever temptations the devil brings against the saints there is power at hand, even a buckler, to parry the blows.

Remember ever — forget never — be comforted ever — to know that Jesus came "that through death he might destroy him that hath the power of death, that is, the devil."

All this brings us now to think of that, another grim reality, which is contrary to us —

VI. DEATH

What spiritual wealth is ours, as pointed out by Paul:

Therefore let no man glory in men. For all things are yours; whether Paul, or Apollos, or Cephas, or the world, or life, or death, or things present, or things to come; all are yours; And ye are Christ's; and Christ is God's (I Corinthians 3:21-23).

Though I walk through the valley of the shadow of death, I will fear no evil. (No sting. No substance. Only a shadow.)

Forasmuch then as the children are partakers of flesh and blood, he also himself took part of the same; that through death he might destroy him that had the power of death, that is, the devil; and deliver them who through fear of death were all their lifetime subject to bondage (Hebrews 2:14, 15).

Let us read Romans 8:38, 39 in reverse order — and this way: "I am persuaded that not any creature, nor depth, nor height, nor things to come, nor things present, nor powers, nor principalities, nor angels, nor life, nor death shall be able to separate us from the love of God, which is in Christ Jesus, our Lord."

"Nor death." Death, if Jesus tarry in His coming, is a stark unwelcome certainty, an often dreaded reality. Death — when diptheria flutters its black wings over the baby cradle. Death — when polio paralyzes the muscles. Death — when fever fires burn in brains and blood channels. Death — when cancer gnaws its relentless way as a worm gnawing at the heart of a rose. Death — when tuberculosis eats up the lungs. Death — when paralysis creeps as moths destroying clothes. Death — when the train turns turtle. Death — when the plane falls. Death — when the auto crashes. Death — when the ship sinks. Death — when the lightning snuffs out life. Death — when earthquake swallows a city. Death — when old age, bit by bit draws us down. Death — expected or unexpected. Death — stalking its way to the door of hut and palace.

But victory can be had over death as expressed in the words of Theodosia Garrison:

> Let me not picture Death as one who stalks a helpless enemy;
> To blot away the sun some day, and lay relentless hands on me.
> Nay, rather, let me think of him as one who in all kindness waits
> At the road's end, when shadows dim, to draw me gently through
>   his gates.
> And lead me, like some kindly host, who gives a long-expected guest
> The comfort that he craves the most — the hospitality of rest.
> So may I think of him each day, while the road shortens mile
>   by mile,
> Guessing the word that he will say, almost familiar with his smile.
> No foe with fury in his breath shall charge me from some
>   ambushed place;
> God grant I make a friend of Death, long, long before I see
>   his face.

Yes, Christ triumphed in death for His people. Let the print of the nails which Thomas saw and which we shall some day see tell it forth. The nails of the cross have ensured for us a nail in His holy place.

> And now for a little space grace hath been shewed from
> the Lord our God, to leave us a remnant to escape, and to
> give us a nail in his holy place that our God may lighten
> our eyes, and give us a little reviving in our bondage
> (Ezra 9:8).

A marginal reading is very beautiful — "a pin that is a constant and sure abode." There can be no change in the mind of the Lord. His decrees are unchangeable, constant, sure. And, as Maclaren says, "While today's health may be tomorrow's sickness, while today's wealth may be tomorrow's poverty, while today's happy companionship of joy may be tomorrow's aching solitude of heart, we know that today's Christ is tomorrow's Christ — the same yesterday, today, forever." And though today's life be tomorrow's death, through Christ we can be "more than conquerors." Amid all the uncertainty about dwelling places upon earth, houses being sold over one's head, people being "read out," great difficulties in finding accommodations, what a mercy and what a joy to remember and to realize that the heavenly abode *is sure*.

How does it come that the people of God have this glorious prospect? Because He, typified by Eliakim, is fastened as a nail in a sure place — and all the vessels of mercy hang upon Him.

> And that he might make known the riches of his glory on
> the vessels of mercy, which he had afore prepared unto
> glory (Romans 9:23).
> And I will fasten him as a nail in a sure place; and he
> shall be for a glorious throne to his father's house (Isaiah
> 22:23).

It was the nails of the cross which did this blessed work. Apart from Calvary, there could have been no sure place, no certain abode — only the blackness of darkness forever. God keep us faithful and zealous of good works until we are gathered together to behold the print of the nails in the hands and the feet of the Christ whom our soul loveth.

Now, let me exhort you that because Christ put away all that was contrary to us, nailing it to His cross, let us put away from our lives all that is contrary to His will.

"For the grace of God that bringeth salvation hath appeared to all men, teaching us that, denying ungodliness and worldly lusts, we should live soberly, righteously, and godly, in this present world; looking for that blessed hope and the glorious appearing of the great God and our Saviour Jesus Christ; who gave Himself for us, that He might redeem us from all iniquity, and purify unto Himself a peculiar people, zealous of good works" (Titus 2:11-14).

Now, praying that you will ponder all the words of this message, I beg you to treasure in your heart the beautiful words of the hymn:

> There was One who was willing to die in my stead,
> That a soul so unworthy might live,
> And the path to the Cross, He was willing to tread,
> All the sins of my life to forgive.
>
> He is tender and loving and patient with me,
> While He cleanses my heart of its dross;
> But "there's no condemnation," I know I am free,
> For my sins have been taken away.
>
> I will cling to my Saviour and never depart —
> I will joyfully journey each day,
> With a song on my lips and a song in my heart,
> That my sins have been taken away.
>
> They are nailed to the cross, they are nailed to the cross,
> O how much He was willing to bear!
> With what anguish and loss, Jesus went to the Cross!
> But He carried my sins with Him there.
>
> *Grant Colfax Tullar*

The Hair of Five

CHAPTER IV

THE HAIR OF FIVE

His hairs were grown . . . like eagle's feathers (Daniel 4:33).
The hairs of his head began to grow (Judges 16:22).
He weighed the hair of his head (II Samuel 14:26).
She did wipe his feet with the hairs of her head (Luke 7:38).
His head and his hairs were white as snow (Revelation 1:4).

About fifty times in the Bible the words "hair," "hairs," and "hairy" are found. But now we give thought to the hair of five persons.

First, the

I. HAIR OF NEBUCHADNEZZAR

This man was one of the greatest and most powerful of the Babylonian kings, the son and successor of Nabapolasser, founder of the Babylonian empire. Nebuchadnezzar reigned in big and glorious Babylon for forty-three years. At this time, all roads — all broad, level, ribbon-like, oft crowded with marching captives from Egypt, Judah, Syria — led to Babylon. These roads were flanked by obelisks, monuments, palaces, temples, gardens — winding up to a dream city built on the site of old Babel's tower. A city it was of one thousand flowered terraces and temple towers, shining in marble and silver, like the stars of heaven, with the hanging gardens, one of the seven wonders of the world, built by the king for his queen.

Under powerful Nebuchadnezzar the city rose to such grandeur, beauty, magnificence, and extent that Herodotus, who visited it 460 B.C. describes it as forming a square of fourteen miles on each side — with walls three hundred and fifty feet high.

Babylon, the metropolis of the world, was, under Nebuchadnezzar, the center of commerce, art, wisdom, wealth, wonders.

Unquestioned was king Nebuchadnezzar's power. "The most high God," said Daniel, "gave Nebuchadnezzar a kingdom, majesty, glory, honour. All peoples, nations, and languages trembled and feared before him. Whom he would he slew; whom he would he kept alive; whom he would he set up; whom he would he put down" (Daniel 5:18, 19). He beseiged and captured Jerusalem. He took the Jews into captivity into Babylon where Jewish hands worked, Jewish brows did sweat, Jewish backs bore burdens for Chaldean comforts and luxuries. "So Judah was carried away out of their land" (II Kings 25:21).

Nebuchadnezzar, starting the final seige of Jerusalem in the ninth year of King Zedekiah, and in his own seventeenth year (586 B.C.) dealt mercilessly with Zedekiah. We read:

> So they took the king, and brought him up to the king of Babylon to Riblah; and they gave judgment upon him. And they slew the sons of Zedekiah before his eyes, and put out the eyes of Zedekiah, and bound him with fetters of brass, and carried him to Babylon (II Kings 25:6, 7).

After burning Jerusalem "the house of the Lord, the kings' house, all the houses of Jerusalem, and every great man's house," Nebuchadnezzar returned to Babylon. Puffed with pride, he sought deification — self deification — as is shown by the erection of the golden image in the plain of Dura:

> Nebuchadnezzar the king made an image of gold, whose height was three-score cubits, and the breadth thereof six cubits: he set it up in the plain of Dura, in the province of Babylon (Daniel 3:1).

The statue was not as tall as the Statue of Liberty — one hundred and fifty one feet high, on a pedestal a hundred and fifty-five feet high, three hundred and six feet in total height. Not as tall as the Colossus of Rhodes — one hundred and six feet high. Not as tall as the Statue of Nero — one hundred and ten feet high. Nebuchadnezzar gave this cruel command concerning the image:

> And whoso falleth not down and worshippeth shall the same hour be cast into the midst of a burning fiery furnace (Daniel 3:6).

Nebuchadnezzar's desire for self-deification and worship was changed to cruelty in the rage and fury with which he commanded the three refusing Hebrews to be burned:

> Then was Nebuchadnezzar full of fury, and the form of his visage was changed against Shadrach, Meshach, and Abednego: therefore he spake, and commanded that they should heat the furnace seven times more than it was wont to be heated (Daniel 3:19).

In his ugly-tempered vanity and pride, the king cursed, killed, oppressed. In his worship of himself, in his demand that others look upon him as a god, he praised himself. An arrogant "I," a strutting "me," a haughty "my" and "mine" were often on his bragging lips. "*I* in *mine* house." "*My* palace." "*I* made a decree."

> The king spake, and said, Is not this great Babylon, that I have built for the house of the kingdom by the might of my power, and for the honour of my majesty? (Daniel 4:30).

Note Nebuchadnezzar's dethronement:

> While the word was in the king's mouth, there fell a voice from heaven, saying, O king Nebuchadnezzar, to thee it is spoken; The kingdom is departed from thee (Daniel 4:31).
>
> But when his heart was lifted up, and his mind hardened in pride, he was deposed from his kingly throne, and they took his glory from him (Daniel 5:20).

And his debasement:

> The same hour was the thing fulfilled upon Nebuchadnezzar: and he was driven from men, and did eat grass as oxen, and his body was wet with the dew of heaven, till his hairs were grown like eagles' feathers, and his nails like birds' claws (Daniel 4:33).
>
> And he was driven from the sons of men; and his heart was made like the beasts, and his dwelling was with the wild asses: they fed him with grass like oxen, and his body was wet with the dew of heaven; till he knew that the most high God ruled in the kingdom of men, and that he appointeth over it whomsoever he will (Daniel 5:21).

Looking at this insane king, "his hairs . . . like eagles' feathers," we learn that "those that walk in pride he (God) is able to abase" (Daniel 4:37), that God can put the bodies of Christ-rejecting men and women in graves — can bring destruction upon all who are God-defiant.

God says: "Pride do I hate" (Proverbs 8:13).

Nebuchadnezzar, even as many in our day, was as void of humility as a frog is of feathers, as a turtle of sheep's wool. "When thou wast little in thine own sight" — such words never applied to him. This *little* man in *big* Babylon could strut sitting down.

The only "i's" in the Bible with a crown are the small ones. The capital "I's" are devoid of any crown. Teaching us what? Teaching that we must walk humbly with God and our fellow men — remembering that God says: "Woe unto the crown of pride" (Isaiah 28:1).

"Pride is not of the Father" (I John 2:16).

The Apostle Peter wrote — by the Holy Spirit: "Be clothed with humility, for God resisteth the proud — and giveth grace to the humble. Humble yourselves therefore under the mighty hand of God that he may exalt you in due time" (I Peter 5:5, 6).

Humbling ourselves, we need to remember Jesus' words: "Learn of me, for I am meek and lowly in heart" (Matthew 11:29).

We are glad to read this about King Nebuchadnezzar's penitent confession and restoration:

> And at the end of the days I Nebuchadnezzar lifted up mine eyes unto heaven, and mine understanding returned unto me, and I blessed the most High, and I praised and honoured him that liveth for ever, whose dominion is an everlasting dominion, and his kingdom is from generation to generation: And all the inhabitants of the earth are reputed as nothing: and he doeth according to his will in the army of heaven, and among the inhabitants of the earth: and none can stay his hand, or say unto him, What doest thou? At the same time my reason returned unto me; and for the glory of my kingdom, mine honour and brightness returned unto me; and my counsellors and my lords sought unto me; and I was established in my kingdom, and excellent majesty was added unto me. Now I Nebuchadnezzar praise and extol and honour the King of heaven, all whose works are truth, and his ways judgment: and those that walk in pride he is able to abase (Daniel 4:34-37).

How blessed the truth that God restores "the years that the locust hath eaten" (Joel 2:25). How comforting to us David's testimony: "He brought me up also out of an horrible pit, out of the miry clay, and set my feet upon a rock, and established my goings. And he hath put a new song in my mouth, even praise unto our God" (Psalm 40:2, 3).

The second one whose hair we are giving thought to is the —

II. HAIR OF SAMSON

> And she made him sleep upon her knees: and she called for a man, and she caused him to shave off the seven locks of his head; and she began to afflict him, and his strength went from him (Judges 16:19).

Much tragedy is in those words that make us think of a man whose history is a history of miracles and prodigies. This man, Samson, held a marvellous hold upon the imaginations of all succeeding generations — because a man of great individual exploits always impresses the modern mind more than the wisest statesmanship or the greatest generalship.

Samson was blessed.

> And the woman bare a son, and called his name Samson: and the child grew, and the Lord blessed him. And the Spirit of the Lord began to move him at times in the camp of Dan between Zorah and Eshtaol (Judges 13:24, 25).

Samson had a good mother. Before his birth his mother was told:

> But thou shalt conceive, and bear a son. Now therefore beware, I pray thee, and drink not wine nor strong drink, and eat not any unclean thing: For, lo, thou shalt conceive, and bear a son; and no razor shall come on his head: for the child shall be a Nazarite unto God from the womb: and he shall begin to deliver Israel out of the hand of the Philistines (Judges 13:3-5).

The dominant idea was consecration. The token of this consecration was unshaven hair. "The child shall be a Nazarite to God from the womb to the day of his death" (Judges 13:7). Devotion to God.

Samson's physical prowess, shown when he, with nothing in his hand, "rent a lion as he would have rent a kid" (Judges 14:6), was a special gift of God.

Samson, the Bible's Hercules, slaughtered, with no one to help him, thousands of Philistines, carried off the gates to cities, pulled down the temples, burned up "the standing corn of the Philistines, both the shocks and standing corn, with the vineyards and olives" (Judges 15:4, 5). He stood and fought when even mighty Judah's tribe ran from the field. He worshiped God while they deserted to idols. All his achievements were wrought because "the Spirit of the Lord came upon him." Moreover, "He Judged Israel in the days of the Philistines twenty years" (Judges 15:20). The exercise of this judicial function called for knowledge, wise judgment, and fidelity to God's law. The national cowardice of Israel and Philistia form the dark outline of his sublime and solitary courage.

Samson was bothered by two women — one his wife, the other Delilah. Truthful is he who describes Delilah in these words: "Ten of the lowest women multiplied by ten gives you a Delilah — a Philistine courtesan, a woman of unholy and persistent desire and devilish deceit. She and honour never met. Her face had alluring beauty. Her heart, dark as a pool at midnight, held viperous treachery. No father has ever given a daughter her name." "Samson saw a woman in Timnath" — and "she pleased him well" (Judges 14:2, 3). That was the first woman in Samson's life.

Concerning the second woman, we read:

"And it came to pass afterwards, that he loved a woman in the valley of Sorek, whose name was Delilah" (Judges 16:4). By subtle blandishments and deceitful aggressiveness, by poutish plaintiveness, she learned from Samson the secret of his strength — his *hair*.

Bothered was Samson by both these women — both women used as tools by the Philistines. His wife, by weeping and nagging for seven days, vexed his soul terribly. And of devilish Delilah, we read:

> And Delilah said unto Samson, Behold, thou hast mocked me, and told me lies: now tell me, I pray thee, wherewith thou mightest be bound (Judges 16:10).

> And it came to pass, when she pressed him daily with
> her words, and urged him, so that his soul was vexed
> unto death; That he told her all his heart, and said unto
> her, There hath not come a razor upon mine head; for
> I have been a Nazarite unto God from my mother's
> womb: if I be shaven, then my strength will go from me,
> and I shall become weak, and be like any other man
> (Judges 16:16, 17).

Samson's strength arose from his relation to God as a Nazarite. The preservation of his hair unshaven was the mark or sign of his Nazariteship — and a pledge on God's part of the continuance of His miraculous spiritual power. If Samson lost this sign, the badge of his consecration, he broke his vow and consequently forfeited the thing signified.

Samson's strength did not reside in his hair, but in keeping his Nazarite vow of which the unshaven head was a token. He was not to yield the members of his body to live after the flesh, that he might be a powerful instrument in the hand of God. This must be a life of discipline and self-control. In this way, he was to be strong in every way in which a man should be strong.

But bothered Samson became a barbered Samson. Delilah called in Satan's barber:

> And she made him sleep upon her knees; and she called
> for a man, and she caused him to shave off the seven
> locks of his head; and she began to afflict him, and his
> strength went from him (Judges 16:19).

Look at the beautiful locks lying on Delilah's floor. See Delilah, her eyes bright as she looked upon her ill-gotten gains — the money the Philistines paid her to entice him. What a sight in this devil's barber shop — a great lion in the net of the hunter!

Samson *blind*. "But the Philistines took him, and put out his eyes" (Judges 16:21). Midnight his forever!

Samson *bound*. "And bound him with fetters of brass; and he did grind in the prison house" (Judges 16:21). Degraded to the state of a beast. Samson the mighty — in shackles!

Samson making *sport*. The Philistines said: "Dagon . . . our god has delivered into our hands our enemy and the destroyer of our country, who slew many of us."

> And it came to pass, when their hearts were merry, that
> they said, Call for Samson, that he may make us sport.
> And they called for Samson out of the prison house;
> and he made them sport: and they set him between
> the pillars (Judges 16:25).

The big crowd in the big temple! Big doings! Big sacrifice to
Dagon. Big praise of their god! Much merry making. Samson,
the one-time judge, now a clown.

> And Samson said unto the lad that held him by the hand,
> Suffer me that I may feel the pillars whereupon the house
> standeth, that I may lean upon them. Now the house
> was full of men and women; and all the lords of the
> Philistines were there; and there were upon the roof about
> three thousand men and women, that beheld while Sam-
> son made sport. And Samson called unto the Lord, and
> said, O Lord God, remember me, I pray thee, and
> strengthen me, I pray thee, only this once, O God, that
> I may be at once avenged of the Philistines for my two
> eyes. And Samson took hold of the two middle pillars
> upon which the house stood, and on which it was borne
> up, of the one with his right hand, and of the other with
> his left. And Samson said, Let me die with the Philistines.
> And he bowed himself with all his might; and the house
> fell upon the lords, and upon all the people that were
> therein. So the dead which he slew at his death were
> more than they which he slew in his life (Judges 16:
> 26-30).

These words of Samson were not a mere vindictive imprecation
— not a mere desire to "get even." He was willing to die if he
could give one last blow to the enemies of God — the oppressors
of God's people. "The house fell upon the lords." These lords
were the leaders, and their destruction has more effect for peace
than anything else, more than any battle.

We need to remember: "Samson, dying with the Philistines,
no more committed suicide than a general when, with certain
death ahead, rushes into the thickest battle, confident that he
will save his country from a hated foe."

That was another day of victory for Samson. It was the day of
conquest also. He came back into favor with God. He came
back into fullness of power. He came back to the overthrow of
God's enemies and the oppression of God's people. Teaching us

what? That the conquered man, the fallen man, can come back to operative and spiritual power. And how? By penitence and prayer.

Of Samson, Dr. B. H. Carroll said: "Samson was a great man and a good man. Samson was a man of intelligence – a poet, a soldier for God. No wonder that the whole world from that dark time until now thinks about Samson."

We think a bit of Samson *buried:*

> Then his brethren and all the house of his father came down, and took him, and brought him up, and buried him between Zorah and Eshtaol in the burying-place of Manoah his father (Judges 16:31).

With his sightless eyes and the hair of his head that began to grow again after he was shaven (Judges 16:22), they buried him. His shoulders that once carried off the Gaza gates are now wrapped in a burial robe. His hands that once so mightily rent open the lion's mouth and wielded instruments of death upon the enemies of God, they folded.

That once strong body, once embraced by Delilah and some other women, is now in the cold arms of Mother Earth. Thank God he came back to God.

His epitaph: "He judged Israel twenty years" (Judges 16:31). And: "What shall I more say? for the time would fail me to tell of Gedeon, and of Barak, and of Samson, and of Jephthae; of David also, and Samuel, and of the prophets: who through faith subdued kingdoms, wrought righteousness, obtained promises, stopped the mouths of lions" (Hebrews 11:32, 33).

Now, considering the hair of another, we think of the –

III. HAIR OF ABSALOM

Think of Absalom's *birth.*

Of the sons born unto David in Hebron, the third son was Absalom – "the son of Maacah, the daughter of Talmai, King of Geshur" (II Samuel 3:3).

Absalom is mentioned in the Bible – not because of his personal character, but because of his kinship to King David. Absalom illustrates the twofold fact that the man of mighty power in statesmanship and usefulness to his generation may bring up a degenerate son — and yet that son enjoys a certain amount of social standing and popular respect on account of the very blood within his veins.

Absalom is more fully reported in the divine record than Amnon, Chileab, and Adonijah, David's other sons — because he attempted to take the reins of government into his own hands. And he came so near success that a full report of Israel's doings involves the record of his attempted leadership. Absalom, son of David and Maacah, proved a bitter disappointment to his father. He was the murderer of his brother, a rebel against government, an opposer of God.

Think of Absalom's *breeding*.

David seems to have shielded and petted his son, letting him grow up without correction. David seems to have catered to Absalom's every desire, not seeming to believe that a spoiled child is destined for much sorrow. We know that in the spoiled child's sorrow, spoilers must share:

> He that spareth his rod hateth his son: but he that loveth
> him chasteneth him betimes (Proverbs 13:24).
> Chasten thy son while there is hope, and let not thy soul
> spare for his crying (Proverbs 19:18).
> Foolishness is bound in the heart of a child: but the rod
> of correction shall drive it far from him (Proverbs 22:15).

Spoiled Absaloms can never become happiness-producing, honor-bestowing sons.

Think of Absalom's *beauty* — of which his *hair* was a part.

> But in all Israel there was none to be so much praised as
> Absalom for his beauty: from the sole of his foot even
> to the crown of his head there was no blemish in him.
> And when he polled his head, (for it was at every year's
> end that he polled it: because the hair was heavy on him,
> therefore he polled it:) he weighed the hair of his head
> at two hundred shekels after the king's weight (II Samuel
> 14:25, 26).

Think, too, of Absalom's *badness*.

"Absalom hated Amnon" (II Samuel 13:22).

And the Apostle John wrote: "Whosoever hateth his brother is a murderer" (I John 3:15).

Note how handsomely beautiful Absalom's badness was manifest:

> And Absalom rose up early, and stood beside the way of the gate: and it was so, that when any man that had a controversy came to the king for judgment, then Absalom called unto him, and said, Of what city art thou? And he said, Thy servant is of one of the tribes of Israel. And Absalom said unto him, See, thy matters are good and right; but there is no man deputed of the king to hear thee. Absalom said moreover, Oh that I were made judge in the land, that every man which hath any suit or cause might come unto me, and I would do him justice! And it was so, that when any man came nigh to him to do him obeisance, he put forth his hand, and took him, and kissed him. And on this manner did Absalom to all Israel that came to the king for judgment: so Absalom stole the hearts of the men of Israel (II Samuel 15:2-6).

What satanic thievery — stealing human hearts! — the hearts of the men of Israel.

What hypocrisy Absalom showed to King David: "Absalom said unto the king, I have vowed unto the Lord in Hebron" (II Samuel 15:8, 9): "For thy servant vowed a vow while I abode at Geshur in Syria, saying, If the Lord shall bring me again indeed to Jerusalem, then I will serve the Lord. And the king said unto him, Go in peace. So he arose, and went to Hebron."

The following words show what a wicked hypocrite Absalom proved himself to be:

> But Absalom sent spies throughout all the tribes of Israel, saying, As soon as ye hear the sound of the trumpet, then ye shall say, Absalom reigneth in Hebron. And with Absalom went two hundred men out of Jerusalem, that were called; and they went in their simplicity, and they knew not anything. And Absalom sent for Ahithophel the Gilonite, David's counsellor, from his city, even from Giloh, while he offered sacrifices. And the conspiracy was strong; for the people increased continually with Absalom. And there came a messenger to David, saying, The hearts of the men of Israel are after Absalom (II Samuel 15:10-13).

Absalom's badness was manifest in the shed blood of thousands — after David made ready to flee from the palace, saying, "Arise, and let us flee; for we shall not else escape from Absalom: make speed to depart, lest he overtake us suddenly, and bring evil upon us, and smite the city with the edge of the sword" (II Samuel 15:14).

> Where the people of Israel were slain before the servants of David, and there was there a great slaughter that day of twenty thousand men. For the battle was there scattered over the face of all the country: and the wood devoured more people that day than the sword devoured (II Samuel 18:7, 8).

And, in a tragic later hour, Absalom's own blood was shed:

> And Absalom met the servants of David. And Absalom rode upon a mule, and the mule went under the thick boughs of a great oak, and his head caught hold of the oak, and he was taken up between the heaven and the earth: and the mule that was under him went away. And a certain man saw it, and told Joab, and said, Behold, I saw Absalom hanged in an oak (II Samuel 18:9, 10).
>
> And he (Joab) took three darts in his hand, and thrust them through the heart of Absalom, while he was yet alive in the midst of the oak. And ten young men that bare Joab's armour compassed about and smote Absalom, and slew him (II Samuel 18:14, 15).

Think of King David's sorrow — after hearing of Absalom's death:

> And the king was much moved, and went up to the chamber over the gate, and wept: and as he went, thus he said, O my son Absalom! my son, my son Absalom! would God I had died for thee, O Absalom, my son, my son (II Samuel 18:33).

Absalom had physical beauty, but there was no beauty to his badness. We need to know that beauty of body is often a medium of temptation.

Think of Goethe, the German philosopher, and Cleopatra, queen of Egypt — the first, kingly in appearance; the second, queenliest queen in feature and form, but both victims of the adversary. Yes, and both playing part of tempter and temptress — touching other characters to tear them down and to bring against them the awful sentence that Jesus once uttered:

> It were better for him that a millstone were hanged about his neck, and he cast into the sea, than that he should offend one of these little ones (Luke 17:2).

Jesus, speaking of beauty, declared that it should not be outward but inward:

> Woe unto you, scribes and Pharisees, hypocrites! for ye make clean the outside of the cup and of the platter, but within they are full of extortion and excess. Thou blind Pharisee, cleanse first that which is within the cup and platter, that the outside of them may be clean also. Woe unto you, scribes and Pharisees, hypocrites! for ye are like unto whited sepulchres, which indeed appear beautiful outward, but are within full of dead men's bones, and of all uncleanness. Even so ye also outwardly appear righteous unto men, but within ye are full of hypocrisy and iniquity (Matthew 23:25-28).

About Absalom 'tis written: "There was no blemish in him." No — no physical blemish. But his face hid the soul of a devil. His hair covered a head that had no thoughts of godliness in it. He was a wolf in an angel's clothing.

Elizabeth Fry, under conviction of sin, knowing that she was offering God pewter and not gold, looked at herself in the mirror and said, with rebuke of her life: "Elizabeth Fry, you are a contemptible small lady — all outside, no inside."

Perhaps, sometimes, weighing ourselves on God's scales, we find ourselves as guilty as Elizabeth Fry adjudged herself.

We find a sense of relief in turning from thinking upon Nebuchadnezzar's hair like eagles' feathers and of Samson snared and sheared by a woman viper and of Absalom whose beautifully hairy head "caught hold of the oak as he was taken up between the heaven and the earth and the mule that was under him went away" (II Samuel 18:9), to think of the —

IV. Hair of Two Women

One woman, a sinner, ministered to Jesus in the Pharisee's house:

> And one of the Pharisees desired him that he would eat with him. And he went into the Pharisee's house, and sat down to meat. And, behold, a woman in the city, which was a sinner, when she knew that Jesus sat at meat in the Pharisee's house, brought an alabaster box of ointment, And stood at his feet behind him weeping, and began to wash his feet with tears, and did wipe them with the hairs of her head, and kissed his feet, and anointed them with the ointment. Now when the Pharisee

> which had bidden him saw it, he spake within himself,
> saying, This man, if he were a prophet, would have
> known who and what manner of woman this is that
> toucheth him: for she is a sinner (Luke 7:36-39).

Luke says: "A woman who was a sinner." The Pharisee said: "What manner of woman! She is a sinner." Jesus said: "Her sins which are many."

> And he said unto her, Thy sins are forgiven. And they
> that sat at meat with him began to say within themselves,
> Who is this that forgiveth sins also? And he said to the
> woman, Thy faith hath saved thee; go in peace (Luke
> 7:48-50).

Think of two deeds of two different women — deeds similar in beauty — two lovely flowers in the vase of love — both women using their hair to minister to Jesus.

The woman who was a sinner washed Jesus' feet with her tears and "did wipe them with the hairs of her head." And Mary of Bethany — sister of Martha and Lazarus — took "a pound of ointment of spikenard, very costly, and anointed the feet of Jesus, and wiped his feet with her hair: and the house was filled with the odour of the ointment" (John 12:3).

The pound was the Latin *libra*, the unit of weight in the Roman empire — slightly over twelve ounces in weight. "Ointment" was an unguent more costly and luxurious than the ordinary olive oil. The attar of roses, made at Ghezipoor in Hindustan, requires four hundred thousand full-grown roses to produce one ounce — and it sells at over one hundred dollars an ounce.

Mary put the equivalent of four million, eight hundred thousand roses on the head and feet of Jesus. "Mary . . . . wiped Jesus' feet with her hair."

But not of the hair of Mary of Bethany will I speak, but of her who was stamped as a sinner. Simon, the Pharisee, was an honest friend of Jesus, not a scornful and supercilious adversary, as were many Pharisees. Simon was gradually emerging from the prejudices of Phariseeism in which he had so long been schooled.

Simon "desired Jesus to eat with him" — and so we have this striking scene in Simon's home. Reclining at the table in a large court, with their feet extending back from the table in the oriental divans, the guests were assembled at meat. Around the walls of the large court a motley crowd sometimes gathered, freely passing through the open doors according to the simple etiquette of an Eastern home. There was no reason why this poor woman who was "a sinner in the city" could not also slip in with the crowd and take her place behind the seated guests. "She stood at his feet behind him — weeping." Satan's soot and smut behind God's snow! Penitential thorn bush and "Lily of the Valley." Devil's cactus plant close by the "Rose of Sharon!" Dirty toy of dirtier men in the presence of holiness.

All that she did was carefully planned by her. Knowing that Christ was to be there, she chose this time to express her love and gratitude. Having heard Him speak gracious words, she, no doubt, looked upon Him with wonder. The Lord Jesus' clearly implies that her love was the result of a great sense of forgiveness. The gift she brought was costly. Perhaps it was the wages of her sin. Surely if ever gift was "tainted," this gift was. But the Lord can accept the gift of the vilest if the gift is accompanied by tears that show that the heart and hands that brought them have been cleansed.

She had meant to be calm and proper in her thank offering, but ere she knew it, a strong feeling had swept away all barriers — and she found her tears would not stay back, but fell in torrents of passionate love and contrition at His feet. Luke says: "She began to wash his feet with tears." Those tears covered His holy feet and made it difficult for her to anoint them as she wished, and had planned. The tears were not in the program. So she loosed her long tresses and with her hair, she wiped away the tear stains from His feet. Then she took the costly ointment and, with many a caress of love, she "kissed his feet and anointed them with the ointment" — and the house was filled with the sweet odor of the oil and the weary feet of Jesus were refreshed.

This woman who was known as a "sinner in the city" kissed

and wiped with her hair the feet of Him who was the "seed of the woman," who was "made of a woman" — as the great Creator honors the feminine creature. On woman, there*by* and there*fore*, was conferred incomparable glory. Jesus, who had the form and flesh of a man, who left His mother, who never espoused a wife, was surrounded all His life, and after His death, by the warmth and sweetness of feminine tenderness.

Simon, whom Jesus had healed of leprosy, gave Jesus no water for His burning, sand-sore feet, but we have the beautiful reality of "woman bedewing His feet with tears, anointing them with tears, anointing them with costly ointment and drying them with the hairs of her head." And all before the nails bruised and pierced them. "Favor is deceitful, and beauty is vain: but a woman that feareth the Lord, she shall be praised. Give her of the fruit of her hands; and let her own works praise her in the gates" (Proverbs 31:30, 31).

She used her hair — woman's glory — to serve the King of Glory. "But if a woman have long hair, it is a glory to her: for her hair is given her for a covering" (I Corinthians 11:15).

She must have combed her hair with delight ever after. How her heart went singing every day, because her sins "which were many" were forgiven. From then on, even until she died, I think — this woman loved Jesus *much,* for *much* she had been forgiven. On the basis of assurance of forgiveness of sins, we should love Jesus *much* — because this is written:

> In whom we have redemption through his blood, even the forgiveness of sins (Colossians 1:14).

And finally we would have you think with us of the —

V. HAIR OF CHRIST

> His head and his hairs were white like wool, as white as snow (Revelation 1:14).

The Apostle John was also beholding the Ancient of Days of Daniel's similar vision.

> I beheld till the thrones were cast down, and the Ancient of days did sit, whose garment was white as snow, and the hair of his head like the pure wool: his throne was like the fiery flame, and his wheels as burning fire (Daniel 7:9).

What John wrote, "His hairs were as white as snow," is in agreement with what Daniel said centuries before: "I beheld . . . the Ancient of days — the hair of his head like pure wool." Both statements speak of Christ's age and agelessness.

Micah wrote:

> But thou, Bethlehem Ephratah, though thou be little among the thousands of Judah, yet out of thee shall he come forth unto me that is to be ruler in Israel; whose goings forth have been from of old, from everlasting (Micah 5:2).

Jesus said: "Before Abraham was I am" (John 8:58). So it is no new Jesus Christ John sees, but the sinless One who is "the same yesterday, today and forever" (Hebrews 13:8). Jesus is no experimenter coming to the crucible, but the aged Christ, with all the wonders and mysteries of ancientness, of antiquity, and things before — the One who is "before all things" (Colossians 1:17), the first born among many brethren (Romans 8:9), the first born of every creature (Colossians 1:15) is the aged Christ. But if I were to tell you that Jesus was one thousand million years old that would give you no adequate idea of Jesus' age and agelessness.

This Jesus is the same Jesus who heard David's prayer, Elijah's solemn call from Carmel for fire from heaven, the leper's cry for cleansing, and the dying thief's cry for mercy. This is the same Jesus who hushed raging Galilee into peace, who broke up the funeral procession at Nain and who has seen every burial since. This same Jesus on whose bosom John leaned, who sat in the Mamertine dungeon, watched the ashes of Wycliff when they were thrown into the river.

This Jesus whom Nebuchadnezzar saw walking with Shadrach, Mechach, and Abednego "in the midst of the fire" (Daniel 3:25) is the same Jesus who stood by Hugh Latimer in the fire and comforted Savonarola burning at the stake. After centuries of sin-pardoning, burden-bearing, wound-healing, sorrow-comforting, Jesus knows how to do such today. You cannot bring Him a new case. He has had one hundred thousand cases of the worst and most desperate — and not by one case has He ever been baffled.

No sin is too horrible for His pardoning grace. No burden is beyond His strength. No wound is beyond His healing. No night is beyond His lightening — because He is an aged Christ. Jesus of the white hair is so sympathetic with all those who have white hair today. If you become weary in life, here is an arm to lean on. If your eyes grow dim, Jesus will pick out the way for you. These words tell what this aged and ageless Christ will do for you:

> I will instruct thee and teach thee in the way which thou
> shalt go: I will guide thee with mine eye (Psalm 32:8).

This aged and ageless Christ will help in youth, will help in old age, from the sunup to the sundown of life. He will help the aged not to be dead before death, a fate much to be shunned, no matter

> How far the gulf stream of Youth may flow,
> Into the Arctic regions of our lives
> Where little else than life itself survives.

The aged and ageless Christ will keep those who are growing old from the tragedy set forth by Chesterfield of himself and his crony, Lord Trawley:

> He said: "Lord Trawley and I have been dead this two
> years, but we do not choose to have it known."

And He will enable us to say singingly:

> Grow old along with me,
> The best is yet to be;
> The last of life for which the first was made . . .
> My times are in God's hands.

But the *white* hairs as pictured in Revelation are a symbol of His *agony*. Luke says: "He was in agony."

Nothing so changes the color of the hair as sorrow, as trouble, as *soul* agony. In Gethsemane, Jesus said: "*My Soul* is exceeding sorrowful unto death" (Matthew 26:38).

Into Gethsemane hours were crowded by prevision, the combined horrors of the cross — its cruelty, shame, physical torment, spiritual tortures. What others had only heard of, Jesus knew. He felt with the greatest intensity the sins of all the world — the most awful results of sin upon the human race. It was the unspeakable sorrow of the world on the most radiant manifestation of love God Himself could make to the human race.

The sins of all the world were, in a mysteriously peculiar way, in crushing accumulation upon His soul — and piled up to heaven like high and heavy mountains on the top of high mountains. Christ's sufferings were infinite, not merely finite, because they had to be satisfaction for our sins, which demand infinite sufferings.

Queen Marie Antoinette came to Paris — greeted by a multitudinous shout, the mightiest Frenchman, her escort. The populace actually tried to unharness the horses from her carriage, that they themselves might draw it. Beautiful in person, beautiful in heart, the whole French nation worshiped her.

A little time passed. We see her on a rough sled drawn to the place of execution — her arms pinioned behind her, the glory of her face extinguished, her husband executed, her children torn from her embrace, the blade of the guillotine sharpening for her neck.

In one night, her hair turned *white.* Surely, our Lord had sorrows enough to whiten His hair. He had dwelt in the palaces of eternity — archangels His body guards, the unfallen ones of heaven glad to draw His resplendent chariot.

But, on earth, He was down on the sled of humanity to the place of execution. His dying drink, vinegar and gall. Forsaken by all, except friends, executioners, and darkness, the black nurse that bent over him. Let the earthquake rumble its dolorous dirge, let the thunder roll at the funeral of God's Son, let the organ of the winds weep and wail His requiem.

> He was wounded for our transgressions.
> He was despised and rejected of men.
> He was bruised for our iniquities.
> He died for the ungodly (for *us*).

Look! You will see "his hair as white as snow." Sorrow and anguish caused by our sins made it so.

Solomon said: "His head is as the most fine gold, his locks are bushy, and black as a raven." But John wrote: "*His head white as snow.*"

And because Jesus sorrowed and suffered unto death, we, through faith in Him, have the supreme blessedness — eternal life.

Blood on Ears and Hands and Toes

Chapter V

BLOOD ON EARS AND HANDS AND TOES

> And Moses . . . brought the ram of consecration . . .
> and he slew it. And Moses took of the blood of it, and
> put it on the tip of Aaron's right ear, and upon the thumb
> of his right hand, and upon the great toe of his right foot
> (Leviticus 8:23).

> And he brought Aaron's sons, and Moses put of the blood
> upon the tip of their right ear, and upon the thumbs of
> their right hands, and upon the great toes of their right
> feet: and Moses sprinkled the blood upon the altar round
> about (Leviticus 8:24).

We have been taught and we believe that Leviticus stands
in the same relation to Exodus that the epistles do to the gospels,
that Exodus is the record of redemption and lays the foundation
of the cleansing, worship, and service of a redeemed people.
"Leviticus gives the detail of the walk, worship, and service of
that people. In Exodus God speaks out of the mount to which
approach was forbidden."

God said to Moses: "The Lord shall come down . . . . upon
Mount Sinai."

> And thou shalt set bounds unto the people round about,
> saying, Take heed to yourselves that ye go not up into
> the mount, or touch the border of it: whosoever toucheth
> the mount shall be surely put to death (Exodus 19:12).

In Leviticus, God speaks out of the tabernacle in which God
dwells in the midst of His people to tell them that which befits
His holiness in their approach *to* and in communion *with* Himself. So says Scofield. Holiness is the keyword of Leviticus —
and occurs eighty-seven times. The key verse of Leviticus is:
"Speak unto all the congregation of the children of Israel, and

101

say unto them, Ye shall be holy: for I the Lord your God am holy" (Leviticus 19:2).

Of the *nine* definite divisions in Leviticus, the third division sets forth matters of consecration — as we find such set forth from chapters eight and nine.

The eighth chapter of Leviticus shows how Aaron and his sons were publicly set apart and inducted into the office of the priesthood. This chapter shows the separation, the decoration, the consecration, and the purification of Aaron and his sons to the priesthood.

Aaron is the only man about whom we have read whose garments were designed and designated by the omniscient God.

> And thou shalt make holy garments for Aaron thy brother for glory and for beauty. And thou shalt speak unto all that are wise hearted, whom I have filled with the spirit of wisdom, that they may make Aaron's garments to consecrate him, that he may minister unto me in the priest's office. And these are the garments which they shall make; a breastplate, and an ephod, and a robe, and a broidered coat, a mitre, and a girdle: and they shall make holy garments for Aaron thy brother, and his sons, that he may minister unto me in the priest's office (Exodus 28:2-4).

Before the garments of glory and beauty were put on, Aaron and his sons were washed together. "And Moses brought Aaron and his sons, and washed them with water" (Leviticus 8:6). Water was a symbol of the Word of God. Washing means applying the Word — applying the truth. Applying the truth and setting apart for a particular service is sanctification.

The washing of Aaron and his sons *together* sets forth *unity* in sanctification — even as Christ and His church are a unit in sanctification before God.

> For both he that sanctifieth and they who are sanctified are all of one: for which cause he is not ashamed to call them brethren (Hebrews 2:11).

For the sake of those cleansed and redeemed by His precious blood — the crimson cash He paid in crucifixion agonies and death — Christ Jesus sanctified Himself, devoted Himself to God and sanctified the saved.

> And for their sakes I sanctify myself, that they also might
> be sanctified through the truth (John 17:19).

Truly, Aaron was a God-clothed man. And in this act of God-designed decoration, we behold our Lord Jesus Christ in typical prefiguration — as many truth lovers have taught us.

Moses, doing what God commanded, dressed Aaron in the eight garments of glory and beauty. He put them on piece by piece — so that they could be seen in all the details of skilled workmanship and surpassing beauty.

On Aaron was put the embroidered linen coat with the linen breeches. He was girdled with the girdle which bound him in with its fineness of texture and perfection of color. Moses put on Aaron the blue robe with its ringing golden bells and pomegranates in their trinity of color. Moses put on the gold ephod, buttoned it on the shoulders with two onyx stones, set the breastplate, and put on the Urim and Thummin — two precious stones signifying light and perfections. Then this was bound to the shoulders with wreathen chains, underneath the ephod at the waist with the curious girdle or belt. Last of all, Moses took the snowy white linen, the costly bussus, wound it fold on fold around his head, making a turban of it. Then he put blue lace on the front of it, and on that fastened the golden plate with the graven words upon it — *"Holiness to the Lord."*

In this manner of investiture, the people saw the intricate worth of these garments of glory and beauty. Thus they beheld Aaron set apart from all others — exalted above the people, yet *for* the people.

The BREASTPLATE signifies the *loving* Christ.

The EPHOD speaks of the *human* and *divine* Christ.

The ROBE speaks of the *heavenly* and *gracious* Christ.

The linen COAT and BREECHES set forth the truth of the *sinless* Christ.

The GIRDLE speaks of the *serving* Christ.

The SHOULDER pieces declare the truth of the *strengthening* and *sustaining* Christ.

The MITRE is emblematic of the *obedient* Christ.

The golden PLATE symbolizes the *holy* Christ.

Thinking of how Aaron, dressed by Moses in garments of glory and beauty, was exalted and set apart *from* all others, exalted *above* the people and yet *for* the people, we say that for two thousand years Jesus, whom God hath highly exalted and to whom God hath given a name which is above every name (Philippians 2), has been set forth in His aloneness upon the consciousness of the world.

The more Jesus is studied, analyzed, the more His character is taken apart, the more His life is submitted to critical analysis, each element of it, like the separate pieces in the garments of glory and beauty, the more it will reveal Christ to be the perfect, the glorious, the beautiful, the wonder of all wonders, perfect man and very God — yea, the verity of God's truth, the beauty of God's holiness, the purity of God's nature, the surety of God's promise, the reality of God's love, the majesty of God's throne, the authority of God's power, the pity of God's heart, the legacy of God's will.

We must not forget, however, that oil was poured on Aaron's head.

> And Moses took the anointing oil, and anointed the tabernacle and all that was therein and sanctified them. And he sprinkled thereof upon the altar seven times, and anointed the altar and all his vessels, both the laver and his foot, to sanctify them. And he poured of the anointing oil upon Aaron's head, and anointed him, to sanctify him (Leviticus 8:10-12).

This oil was not only an anointing for service, but the seal of the redemption that came by the blood — the blood of Christ.

The centuries from Adam to Christ were crimson with the blood of innocent victims killed as types of the slain Lamb of God. The diversified, systematic sacrifices of the Jews, like finger posts along the highway of time, pointed worshipers to a sacrificial Saviour. Significant shadows of redemptive entity still ahead, adumbrations of a substance yet to come, by the blood of a thousand altars, these sacrifices, elemental, preparatory, rudimentary, preliminary, introductory, pointed to Christ, the propellent center to which the faith of mankind before and since gravitated.

There is a theology that counts such truth too vulgar to be attributed to divine ordinances, but to be viewed as belonging to the grosser mind of man in his unrefined stages of development. But men label God and label the Bible a lie by believing anything contrary to the truth, or by preaching or by teaching anything contrary to the truth that the blood stream was ordained of God. The promise to fallen men in Eden means Christ. All the ceremonies of Judaism mean Christ. The music of Israel's sweetest harps means Christ. The light that burns in prophecy means Christ.

Now, let us think of the —

I. BLOOD APPLIED

The blood of the sacrifice was applied to Aaron and his sons. The blood was put upon the tip of the right ear, upon the thumb of the right hand, and upon the big toe of the right foot. This was the three-fold consecration of the holy priesthood.

What was the meaning of all this? The meaning was simple enough. It meant the *hearing* had been ceremonially purchased by the blood and was now solemnly and individually consecrated to God. It meant the *service* had been ceremonially purchased by the blood and was now solemnly and individually dedicated and consecrated to God. It meant the *walk* of the priests had been ceremonially purchased by the blood and was now solemnly and individually consecrated to God. This old enactment exactly represents my own dedication, our own dedication, to the service of God and of our fellowmen.

The touch of sacrificial blood on the ear, and hand, and foot seemed to say, and did say: You have been redeemed for this one end that you may be holy servants of a holy God. You have been redeemed that you may surrender to Him every faculty,

every organ, every power. Your whole self from head to foot is
to be your Lord's. If you have been redeemed by the "precious
blood of Christ," it is only that you may serve in newness of
spirit, both the God above you and your brethren at your side.

Our hearing, our service, our walk — all for Christ. For us who
believe all these, even as all members of our mortal bodies, belong to Christ Jesus who has purchased us, has bought us from
Satan's slave markets of sin and bondage by His own precious
blood — and from whom we have this urging through the
Apostle Paul: "I beseech you therefore, brethren, by the mercies
of God, that ye present your bodies a living sacrifice, holy,
acceptable unto God, which is your reasonable service" (Romans
12:1).

Yes, and from whom also, through the same great apostle, we
have this exhortation:

> Let not sin therefore reign in your mortal body, that
> ye should obey it in the lusts thereof. Neither yield ye
> your members as instruments of unrighteousness unto sin:
> but yield yourselves unto God, as those that are alive
> from the dead, and your members as instruments of right-
> eousness unto God (Romans 6:12, 13).

Let us think of the application of the —

II. BLOOD ON THE EAR

"Moses put of the blood on the tip of the right ear."

God, knowing that we know that the ear is the mysterious
home of reverberations and echo, wants our ears to be instruments of righteousness.

The *ear* is the Grand Central depot of sound. The ear, the
headquarters to which there come dispatches, part of the way
by cartilage, part of the way by air, part of the way by bone,
part of the way by nerve — the slowest dispatch coming into the
ear at the speed of eleven hundred feet per second.

The *ear*, small instrument of music on which is played all the
music you ever hear — from the grandeurs of summer thunder-
storm to the softest breathings of a flute. Small instrument of
hearing only one quarter of an inch of surface — with the thin-

ness of one two-hundred-and-fiftieth part of an inch, and that thinness divided into three layers.

In the *ear* there is the musical staff — lines, spaces, bars, rest.

The *ear* — a delicate bridge leading from the outside *natural* world to the inside *spiritual* world. We see the abutment of this bridge at this end, but the fog of an uplifted mystery hiding the abutment at the other end of the bridge.

The *ear* — wonderful whispering gallery of the soul.

Oh, the *ear* — the God-honored ear, grooved with divine sculpture, poised with divine gracefulness, upholstered with curtains of divine embroidery, corridored with divine carpentry, pillared with divine architecture, chiseled in bone of divine masonry, conquered by processions of divine marshaling — as Talmadge taught.

The *ear!* None but God could plan it; none but God could build it; none but God could work it; none but God could understand it; none but God could keep it.

The *ear* — more wonderful than any arch man ever lifted. More wonderful than any transept window man ever illumined. More wonderful than any Corinthian column man ever crowned. More wonderful than any Gothic cloister man ever elaborated.

The *ear* — more mystifying than any circular stairway ever invented. More majestic than any stone gable ever put in place; more solemnizing than any ocean depth ever fathomed. Blood on the ear with its arches, blood on the ear with its walls, blood on the ear with its floors, blood on the ear with its canals, blood on the ear with its aqueducts, galleries, intricacies, convolutions, and divine machinery.

Because of the blood upon our ear, we are to recognize our hearing does not belong to ourselves. We have no right to listen as it may please us. There are things which, if we permit them to enter the ear, will pass into the mind, poison it, and paralyze all activities for Christ. There is even more peril in listening than in looking and seeing. We are to have the consecrated ear, ever open to the heavenly voice, but closed to the earthly ones that would call us away from truth and godliness — an ear sensitive to the quiet whispers of the spirit, which a dull ear will wholly miss. We are to have an ear gladly listening to the tale of sorrow or distress that comes from the lips of any sufferer or sinner at our side. We are, therefore, called upon to be careful not only as to how we hear but as to what we hear. "And he said unto them, Take heed *what* ye hear!" (Mark 4:24). "Take heed, therefore, *How* ye hear!" (Luke 8:18).

The blood upon the ear tells us He claims our ears that they may hear Him speak, listen to His words, give attention to His message.

Wherefore, it is written: "Who hath ears to hear, let him hear" (Matthew 13:9).

Blood on the tip of the right ear meant that the priest was to listen to only one voice — was to be keenly sensitive to God's voice only — no matter how many clamorous voices were speaking in whispers or in shouts. All believers are kings and priests unto God — through Christ Jesus who loved them and washed, or loosed, them from their sins in His own blood (Revelation 1:5, 6).

And God says to believers what He said to the three disciples on the mountain of transfiguration glory: "This is my beloved Son in whom I am well pleased; *hear* ye him" (Matthew 17:5).

A blood-anointed ear is required to hearken to divine communications. No other ear can hear divine communications. No other ear is familiar with God's divine communication. No other ear is familiar with the divine voice. No other ear is able to understand the language of heaven or the voice that speaks in Holy Scriptures.

God says: "But the natural man receiveth not the things of the Spirit of God: for they are foolishness unto him: neither can he know them, because they are spiritually discerned" (I Corinthians 2:14). So, do not expect the natural man to find pleasure in the voices of the Scriptures. Do not expect the unregenerate scholar to know the simplest truths of divine revelation. There is no blood upon the ear. That is why some scholars do not see at the end of the microscope God's infinitesimal care. That is why many, with college diplomas, do not see at the end of the telescope God's infinite greatness.

If scholars do not see God's immutable ways in the sciences and mathematics; if scholars do not, in the flowers of botany and the sweetness of music, become acquainted with God's ineffable beauty; if scholars do not find in the rocks testimony of God's incomprehensible agelessness, it is because there is no blood on the ear. Unless there is blood on the ear, no man can obey these words:

> He that hath an ear, let him hear what the Spirit saith unto the churches; To him that overcometh will I give to eat of the tree of life, which is in the midst of the paradise of God (Revelation 2:7).

We read: "We have heard with our ears" (Psalm 44:1).

Workers with the deaf say that the child who is hard of hearing is the victim of more misunderstanding than any other child. Often he is ashamed to acknowledge that he cannot hear and he is thought to be stupid, when he simply cannot hear what is said to him. It is the same with those who are spiritually deaf; for there are those who are so framed that they have very little sense of spiritual things. The idea of God is vague in their minds. Christ means little to their soul. The Holy Spirit is a mere name to them. The ears of their souls are stopped up.

"And the ear is first anointed because one must first hear the Word and through it become instructed in the things of Christ, before one can intelligently act in those things or walk worthy of them!"

Now, we think of —

III. BLOOD UPON THE THUMB OF THE RIGHT HAND

"Moses put the blood upon the thumb of the right hand." Thus God bids us to use our hands in His service. This means that we should, with purposed consecration, pray:

> Take my hands and let them move
> At the impulse of thy love.

To handle holy things the blood-sprinkled hand alone is worthy.

For the worship and service of the heavenly sanctuary, to which we belong, it only is competent. Other hands, however morally clean, would but defile. "The precious blood" upon our hands has set them apart to God to be occupied with His affairs, and it makes them both worthy and competent for whatever priestly service he may appoint for them.

A consecrated hand is a hand of ready help; a hand of generous compassion, a hand of strong uplifting for the fallen and the poor. It is a hand of strength "stretched out to wrestlers with the troubled sea!"

A consecrated hand means to give ourselves to Him for His service; to hand ourselves over to Him completely for His use of us. It means we must never come before Him with an empty hand; always and under all circumstances we must come with something in our hand for Him — some service accomplished and handed to Him or some gift presented to Him!

Hear what the Scripture saith: "For Moses said, Consecrate yourselves today to the Lord!" (Exodus 32:29).

Literally rendered that means, "Fill your hands this day to the Lord." This is the actual meaning of the words used in these instances. It means "to fill the hand!" That is God's concept of consecration — coming into His presence with something in your hands.

David said: "Who then is willing to consecrate his service this day unto the Lord?" (I Chronicles 29:5). Meaning: "Who then is willing to *fill his hand* with service this day unto the Lord?" Exodus 23:15; Exodus 34:20: "And none shall appear before me empty."

A noted journalist wrote: "The greatest word in the English language is SERVICE. This is true; and the hands are largely the means by which this service is rendered!"

The hands of the ARTIST are skilful to serve mankind through the medium of beautiful pictures. The hands of the MUSICIAN are delicately sensitive that they may serve mankind through the medium of inspiring music. The hands of the SCULPTOR are triumphantly skillful to serve mankind by raising "from the sterile womb of stone children unto God." The hands of the LABORER are scarred and hard that they may serve mankind through the medium of manual labor. The hands of the doctor and surgeon are wonderfully sensitive and accurate that they may serve mankind through the medium of medical and surgical treatment. The hands of the MOTHER are soiled and worn with the loving work of the household.

We would that the hands made into fists to strike others had the touch of blood upon them. We would that grasping hands, always open to get and never to give liberally, had the touch of blood upon them. We would that the cruel hands of the world, so careless and inconsiderate, had the touch of blood as did Aaron's thumb — and thus be blest with gentleness.

We would that the scornful hands of men the world over, so ready to throw stones of hate, were touched with blood as were the thumbs upon the right hands of Aaron and his sons.

We would that all the hands of all of us had the touch of blood upon them as had the thumb of the right hands of the priests. Then all hands would be the servants of loving wills, the representatives of kindly thought, the tender ambassadors of great hearts, the messengers of God's love and God's grace.

It was a glorious day in the land of Burma when John E. Clough and Lyman Jewett led down into the baptismal waters in a single day two thousand two hundred and twenty-two believers to bury them with Christ in baptism; and surely that was a harvesting season when during the single year of 1878, ten thousand people were baptized on that mission field. But go back fifty years and get the picture of the lonely plowman and his suffering companion, the heroine of Ava. For seven years Adoniram Judson toiled on without seeing any fruitage of his labors, sustained only but sufficiently by the promises of God. And through what trials, hardships and sufferings he and his delicate companion passed in those years of plowing, harrowing and seed-sowing which were to bring forth such a rich harvest in later years. Behold Judson, unjustly cast into a foul prison, languishing therein for months, chained to other prisoners, stripped of most of his clothing, forced to march bareheaded and barefooted under the heat of a torrid sun, his feet torn and blistered, driven by the lash of slaves, himself so exhausted that he would have fallen down and died but for the timely and kindly aid of a Bengalee servant; his wife with infant in arms trying to follow after, to minister, to help if she might, distracted and intrigued against, herself stricken with illness and her babe starving; Judson given a degree of freedom, going from hut to hut begging for his famishing babe a little nourishment from the breasts of native mothers, and you have a picture of the hardships, the labors, the sufferings, the sacrifices of those whose mission it is to go before and to prepare the way for the inheritance of a rich harvest of souls.

The point I am making is, the others who labored had the hard part, the difficult part. We who enter in, who reap the results of their tearful labors, while elated with joy to be reapers, should remember with gratitude, with deepest appreciation, with sincere humility of mind, that greatest praise and greatest honor belong to the toilers who went before.

All honor and gratitude to those, too, who had the touch of the blood upon their ears, so that they listened to the voice of God. There was the touch, too, of the blood upon the hands — so that they were found serving faithfully the Christ whose hands were nailed to Calvary's cross for them — even for us all.

And this brings us to see to it that the blood is upon our hands. Yea, by Christ's hands touching the eyes of the blind into sight, may our hands be yielded unto God as instruments of righteousness.

By Christ's hands touching deaf ears into hearing, touching the fevered brow into coolness, may our hands be hands serving in sympathy. By Christ's hands reached out to sinking Peter on the water, let our hands be reached out to men and women who are down — even if they be in the gutter.

By Christ's hands placed with healing upon the loathesome leper, let not your hands draw back in revulsion from tasks that are not pleasant, even though essential.

By Christ's hands breaking bread for hungry multitudes, may we see to it that our hands are held out with food for the hungry — satisfying the poor with bread (Psalm 132:15) — so that we will never be found guilty under the indictment contained in the words of Eliphaz: "Thou hast not given water to the weary to drink, and thou hast withholden bread from the hungry" (Job 22:7).

By Christ's hands placed blessingly upon little children (Matthew 19:15), let us minister helpfully to little children — remembering the words of Jesus: "Inasmuch as ye have done it unto one of the least of these . . . ye have done it unto me" and "Inasmuch as ye did it *not* to one of the least of these, ye did it not to me" (Matthew 25:40, 45).

By Christ's hands plying the scourge upon the hucksters and herds in the temple, let us see to it that we use our hands as pens that write against wicked forces, as cudgels that break down ramparts of evil — always working for what the devil is against, always active against what Satan is for.

Behold the hands of Christ spiked to Calvary's cross. His hands set the pillars of the earth in their sockets and drew the blue curtains of the night across the windows of heaven and pinned them together with clusters of stars. His hands put the planets in space, so that for ages they have been following their orbits with meticulous accuracy — not one second behind nor one second ahead of the Christ-appointed schedules. His hands laid the first foundations of the waters. Yes, take a look at Christ's hands, *holy* hands, black from the blows of the bruising hammers — hands broken with nails, stained with the sacred oozings of His precious blood. Look gratefully at His hands straining painfully under the weight of His body — while every breath He drew was a pang of pain, while every heart beat was a throb of agony. May our looks at Christ's hands make us earnestly say:

> Lord, Lord,
> Take my hands and let them move
> At the impulse of Thy love.
> Lord, when I am weary with toiling
> And burdensome seem Thy commands;

> If my load should lead to complaining,
> Lord, show me Thy hands;
> Thy nail-pierced hands,
> Thy cross-torn hands,
> My Saviour, show me Thy hands.

Now consider the —

IV.   BLOOD UPON THE GREAT TOE

"Moses took of the blood and put it upon the great toe of the right foot."

The blood upon the great toe of the right foot to make it fit for treading in the holiest and for walking before God in God's love and fear. No other can approach God's dwelling place. Blood answers blood. We read about what took place on the Day of Atonement. Blood was sprinkled seven times before God's throne inside the vail.

> And the priest that is anointed shall bring of the bullock's blood to the tabernacle of the congregation: And the priest shall dip his finger in some of the blood, and sprinkle it seven times before the Lord, even before the vail. And he shall put some of the blood upon the horns of the altar which is before the Lord, that is in the tabernacle of the congregation, and shall pour out all the blood at the bottom of the altar of the burnt offering, which is at the door of the tabernacle of the congregation (Leviticus 4:16-18).

There we behold our perfect standing ground in His presence. There the blood-sprinkled foot may stand.

The blood on the toe means the consecration of the walk before God. The blood means we should be found walking before God, walking in integrity, walking uprightly, walking humbly with God, walking not after the flesh but after the Spirit, walking by faith, walking circumspectly, walking worthy of the Lord — as we are urged to do in God's Word.

Such is to be our walk as those who profess the name of the Lord and own His blood as having all purchasing rights upon us. As Christians we are to live and serve as those who have no initial claims upon ourselves. We strive earnestly to make our walk and conversation glorify Him who has all purchased and invested rights in us. We shall not hesitate to testify that His out-poured blood for us requires that we shall walk as those who seek to walk worthily before men and before God, remembering that we are not our own.

Blood on the *ear*. Blood on the *thumb*. Blood on the big *toe*. How perfect a picture this is of our great Lord Jesus Christ! His ear was ever listening for His Father's voice — ever keenly sensitized to the cry of the needy. His hands were ever busy in the gracious work of ministry to the blind, the deaf, the dumb, the leprous, the helpless, the starving, the devil-possessed, the diseased and the crippled. His feet, carrying Him over the rough and rocky roads, wearied frequently. But he was never too weary to speak a saving word as He did at Jacob's well.

Surely, it was this vision of Christ Jesus which the great Apostle Paul had ever before him when, seeking zealously to magnify the name of Jesus, he wrote: "I magnify mine office" (Romans 11:13). "According to my earnest expectation and my hope, that in nothing I shall be ashamed, but with all boldness, as always, so now also Christ shall be magnified in my body, whether by life or by death" (Philippians 1:20).

"By life! By death!" The second of these alternatives is sometimes easier than the first. To die a martyr's death is not so difficult as to live a consecrated, definitely-devoted, Christ-honoring life — to be "always bearing about in the body the dying of the Lord Jesus, that the life also of Jesus might be made manifest in our body" (II Corinthians 4:11).

Yes, there is quite a difference in dying in a few minutes with the head beneath the guillotine blade, or by rifle bullets before a firing squad, or on a bayonet's point and in living greatly day by day under boresome grind, under heavy burdens, under bitter experiences, under wearisome responsibilities, amid environments that are repulsive where sacrifices are necessary for the support of others and for the achievement of worthy goals.

Our ears. Our hands. Our feet. Our *ears* that gladly hear the blessed words: "I have redeemed thee" — how can they listen with pleasure to any blasphemous utterances, slanderous words, ribald jests, or falsehoods? We should remember ever these words: "A wicked doer giveth heed to false lips: and a liar giveth ear to a naughty tongue" (Proverbs 17:4).

And we should be warned by these words: "He that turneth away his ear from hearing the law, even his prayer shall be abomination" (Proverbs 28:9).

And we should be obedient to these words: "Incline your ears to the words of my mouth" (Psalm 78:11).

Kitty McKeever is the chief telephone operator at Kings Features Syndicate of New York City. Her friends say she never forgets a voice although she handles about two thousand calls a day. Such voice memory is exceptional. But there is one voice we should always "know" regardless of how many voices we are unable to recall. That is the voice of the Good Shepherd, the Lord Jesus Christ.

"His sheep know His voice" (John 10:4). He speaks to them through His Word by His Spirit. What a grand thing to know His voice: in salvation, when He says, "Come unto me" (Matthew 11:28). In fellowship, when He says, "I will never leave thee" (Hebrews 13:5). In guidance when He says, "Follow Me" (Matthew 4:19). In tribulation when He says: "Be of good cheer" (Matthew 14:27). In communion, when He says, "In remembrance of Me" (I Corinthians 11:24, 25). In service, when He says, "Serve Me" (John 12:26). In anticipation when He says: "I will come again" (John 14:3).

Our *hands* that take unto them the emblems of Christ's broken body and shed blood when we observe the Lord's Supper — how can they seize any sinful thing, or do things that hurt rather than help? How can we, knowing the usefulness of our hands, use them in careless ways — to receive bribes, to do evil with both hands earnestly (Micah 7:3), to keep them idle when they should be diligent in work, to stretch them out with scorners (Hosea 7:5), to strengthen hands of evil doers? (Jeremiah 23:14).

Our feet. These feet that enable us to carry our bodies wheresoever we will, that carry us to the house of work — how can they carry us on other days to places where God is dishonored and

His servants condemned, and His laws trampled under foot —
with feet that run to evil? (Isaiah 59:7). How we need to ponder
the paths of our feet. Knowing that we speak with our feet
(Proverbs 6:13), we should never, as does the wicked woman,
have feet that go down to death (Proverbs 5:5), never believing
that "he that hasteth with his feet sinneth" (Romans 19:2).

As those who claim to love and follow Jesus who walked in
blessed benediction among men, we should walk circumspectly,
redeeming the time.

We need to pray:

> Take my life and let it be
> Consecrated, Lord, to Thee;
> Take my hands and let them move
> At the impulse of Thy love.
> Take my feet and let them be
> Swift and beautiful for Thee.

What Jesus Claimed for Himself

CHAPTER VI

WHAT JESUS CLAIMED FOR HIMSELF

There once walked on earth a Person — different from all other persons — the most wonderful Man of all history — "the vox humana in all music, the line of grace in all sculpture, the most exquisite blending of lights and shadows in all paintings, the acme of all climaxes, the dome of all cathedraled grandeurs, and the peroration of all language."

Jesus, the verity of God's truth, the beauty of God's holiness, the purity of God's nature, the reality of God's love, the surety of God's promise, the pity of God's heart, the legacy of God's will, is greater than anything He is ever likened to — something far more than the most illustrious in the census of the world. Human language falls short of expressing all that He is — even as a teacup lacks capacity to hold Niagara Falls. He stands alone, august, unique, supreme — the Fact of facts. All comparisons, all similes, all metaphors just skirt the edges of the glory of this matchless One in whom all sanctities and sufferings unite. Christ Jesus, our Lord, the loftiest ideal of all literature, the highest personality of all philosophies, the supremest problem of all critics, the fundamental doctrine of all Bible-true theology, the cardinal necessity of all ages, was, and is, the superlative of anything high and holy which men choose to call Him.

Believing this, it is tremendously important that we should know what Jesus Himself claimed for Himself — this great Man who was ever "tender without being weak, strong without being coarse, lowly without being servile, mighty in His convictions without being intolerant, enthusiastic but never fanatical, ever holy but never Pharisaic, passionate for the truth but never tainted with prejudice — never making a false step, never betrayed into an error of judgment, never striking a jarring note, never speaking a false word, never maintaining a cowardly silence when He should have spoken."

Without conscious self-assertion and self-expression — speaking as never man spake (John 7:46). Never giving evidence of being egotistical, by word or act or attitude, Jesus made and met claims that no other scholar or philosopher or teacher or ruler could make.

All that the wisest of men, with weightiest of words, can say for Jesus and about Jesus can not equal in weight and wonder what Jesus, Son of Man without sin and Son of God with power, claimed for Himself — showing that Jesus is to history's best and greatest character as light to darkness, as blessing to cursing, as holiness to sin, as music to discordant noise, as heaven to earth, as life to death. Jesus, claiming that He was the main theme of the Bible (John 5:39), by indirect testimony and by direct testimony, made great claims for Himself. By indirect testimony, without pointedly saying that He was God, or the Son of God, He claimed distinctions and powers which could be predicated to no man. By direct testimony, He not only claimed divine power and divine rank, but repeatedly and definitely said that He was God, or the Son of God.

As have written others, as have spoken others, we will give some of both claims — the direct claims and the indirect claims Jesus made concerning Himself.

Jesus claimed —

I. PRE-EXISTENCE

"In the beginning God created" (Genesis 1:1). By whom? "All things were made by him (Jesus); and without him was not anything made that was made" (John 1:3).

Paul said: "And to make all men see what is the fellowship of the mystery, which from the beginning of the world hath been hid in God, who created all things by Jesus Christ" (Ephesians 3:9).

John the Baptist, six months older than Jesus as a babe, definitely testified: "He was before me" (John 1:15).

Abraham lived close to twenty-three hundred years before Jesus, yet Jesus, in verbal warfare with his malicious enemies, said: "Your father Abraham rejoiced to see my day: and he saw it, and was glad. Then said the Jews unto him, Thou are not yet fifty years old, and hast thou seen Abraham? Jesus said unto them, Verily, verily, I say unto you, Before Abraham was, I am" (John 8:56-58).

Not Time but Eternity gives expanse for Him who was "in the beginning" — whenever that beginning was. Micah knew of Jesus' pre-existence:

> But thou, Bethlehem Ephratah, though thou be little among the thousands of Judah, yet out of thee shall he come forth unto me that is to be ruler in Israel; whose goings forth have been from of old, from everlasting (Micah 5:2).

And Jesus, claiming that He came down from heaven, "not to do mine own will, but the will of Him that sent me" (John 6:38), testified that He was with God, and was God, before the morning stars serenaded the advent of this infant earth as it lay "wrapped in swaddling clothes of light in the arms of the great Jehovah."

> And now, O Father, glorify thou me with thine own self with the glory which I had with thee before the world was (John 17:5).
> Father, I will that they also, whom thou hast given me, be with me where I am; that they may behold my glory, which thou hast given me: for thou lovedst me before the foundation of the world (John 17:24).

Thus we see that Jesus was coexistent, coessential, coeternal, coequal with God. "The Father and I are *one*" (John 10:30).

Jesus claimed a —

II. SUPERNATURAL BIRTH

As old as God, His Heavenly Father, and ages older than Mary, His mother, Jesus said to man: "Ye are from beneath; I am from above: ye are of this world; I am not of this world" (John 8:23).

Jesus contrasts the coming into the world of all others with His own coming into the world. He was an uncreated divine Being — the "only begotten Son" (John 3:16) — "God manifest in the flesh" (I Timothy 3:16). Therefore, supernatural manifestations must have gone along with His being "made flesh."

In the Garden of Eden, God took from the body of man a motherless woman. In the cattle barn in Bethlehem, God took from the body of woman a fatherless Man.

And Jesus' supernatural birth is the Alpha of our Christian faith. Let that be accepted and the whole alphabet follows as a matter of course. Deny and reject that truth and, like a planet that leaves its orbit, there is no telling where unbelief will carry folk. The virgin birth is the seal of the Father's approval affixed to the claims of Jesus as His Only-begotten Son. Jesus' birth into our world by virgin womb was a translation at the same time it was an incarnation. It was a transfer of His person from a previous condition of existence to an earthly one. It was His being clothed upon with humanity's nature. He said: "A body hast thou prepared me" (Hebrews 10:5).

Jesus claimed —

III. SINLESSNESS

Preposterous would it be for any human to claim sinlessness. But Jesus, always in perpetual, undeviating, unremitting fellowship with God, readily claimed utter sinlessness. "Which of you convinceth me of sin? And if I say the truth, why do ye not believe me?" (John 8:46).

In Jesus there was no sin — in His mouth no guile. "Christ . . . who did no sin, neither was guilt found in his mouth" (I Peter 2:22). All skeptical microscopes of scrutiny find Him — always and everywhere — wearing nothing but "the white flower of a blameless life." All infidelic telescopes of observation have found in Jesus no taint of sin. Atheistic X-rays of inspection find no flaw or fault in Jesus who was incarnate holiness, who illustrated in His life every doctrine of His heavenly mind. All agnostics, with spectographic investigations, find that temptations never loosened in Him a moral fibre and circumstances left no fingerprints upon His character. All the accusations of His enemies reveal in Jesus a moral earnestness that burned at white heat. Guilty of nothing, ashamed of nothing, regretting nothing, Jesus never knew the humiliation of a moral fall. He had no weakness. Across the ages, we still hear the voice of God as it was heard at the baptism in the Jordan: "This is my beloved Son in whom I am well pleased" (Matthew 3:17).

The writer of the book of Hebrews, bearing testimony to the truth of Jesus' sinlessness, wrote:

> Seeing then that we have a great high priest, that is passed into the heavens, Jesus the Son of God, let us hold fast our profession. For we have not an high priest which can not be touched with the feeling of our infirmities; but was in all points tempted like as we are, yet without sin (Hebrews 4:14, 15).

Jesus abounded in prayer — sometimes spending whole nights in prayer. But in none of His praying was there any suggestion of sin or any indication of repentance. He claimed absolute exemption from the experiences and indulgencies of humanity in sin. Jesus said: "And he that sent me is with me: the Father hath not left me alone; for I do always those things that please him" (John 8:29). There, in those words, we find unquestioned perfection.

Jesus claimed —

IV. OMNIPOTENCE

We read: "And Jesus came and spake unto them, saying, All power is given unto me in heaven and in earth" (Matthew 28:18). We inevitably think of Jesus when we read Isaiah's words:

> Who hath measured the waters in the hollow of his hand, and meted out heaven with the span, and comprehended the dust of the earth in a measure, and weighed the mountains in scales, and the hills in a balance? Who hath directed the Spirit of the Lord, or being his counsellor hath taught him? With whom took he counsel, and who instructed him, and taught him in the path of judgment, and taught him knowledge, and shewed to him the way of understanding? Behold, the nations are as a drop of a bucket, and are counted as the small dust of the balance: behold, he taketh up the isles as a very little thing (Isaiah 40:12-15).

Not only did Jesus claim omnipotence by assertion, but by demonstration — in working miracles. "If I do not the works of my Father, believe me not" (John 10:37). "Believe me that I am in the Father, and the Father in me: or else believe me for the very works' sake" (John 14:11).

We have no greater evidence of the Deity of Christ than that of His manifested power. To enumerate all cases would fill pages.

He had power over diseases — divers diseases. "And Jesus went about all the cities and villages, teaching in their synagogues, and preaching the gospel of the kingdom, and healing every sickness and every disease among the people" (Matthew 9:35). As to human beings, Jesus had power over matter — healing instantly ten decaying lepers.

> And as he entered into a certain village, there met him ten men that were lepers, which stood afar off: and they lifted up their voices, and said, Jesus, Master, have mercy on us. And when he saw them, he said unto them, Go shew yourselves unto the priests. And it came to pass, that, as they went, they were cleansed (Luke 17:12-14).

And power over mind. The lunatic brought to Jesus was healed "from that hour."

> Lord, have mercy on my son: for he is lunatick, and sore vexed: for ofttimes he falleth into the fire, and oft into the water . . . And Jesus rebuked the devil; and he departed out of him: and the child was cured from that very hour (Matthew 17:15, 18).

Another desperate case we know. "And they come to Jesus, and see him that was possessed with the devil, and had the legion, sitting, and clothed, and in his right mind: and they were afraid" (Mark 5:15).

And, as to the human body, Jesus had power over *nerves*. Four men were needed to carry the man sick of the palsy to Jesus.

> And they come unto him, bringing one sick of the palsy, which was borne of four. I say unto thee, Arise, and take up thy bed, and go thy way into thine house. And immediately he arose, took up the bed, and went forth before them all; insomuch that they were all amazed, and glorified God, saying, We never saw it on this fashion (Mark 2:3; 11, 12).

Jesus gave the command. And immediately — as quickly as the lightning flashes in a storm cloud — instead of the man lying on the bed, the bed is on the man, and the man is glorifying God, even as "all were amazed and glorified God."

Jesus, His claims ever factual and never fanciful, could interfere with the harmonious functions of natural law — even as Jesus is necessary to guarantee the harmonious functions of all law.

We read of His restraining power.

> And he said unto them, Where is your faith? And they being afraid wondered saying one to another, What manner of man is this? for he commandeth even the winds and water, and they obey him (Luke 8:25).

We read of His transmuting power — changing one substance into another substance, by a word. Had He yielded to Satan's suggestion, He could have changed stones into bread (Matthew 4:3). We read of how it did please Him at the marriage feast at Cana of Galilee to turn one hundred twenty gallons of a substance named "water" into an entirely different substance called "wine." It was so effectively done that when the governor of the feast had tasted the water that was made wine, he said: "Thou hast kept the good wine until now" (John 2:6-10).

Jesus had destroying power — power to "destroy both body and soul" (Matthew 10:28). This power He used against the barren fig tree, saying: "Let no fruit grow on thee henceforward forever." His blighting the fig tree with a few words caused His disciples to be amazed and to say: "How soon is the fig tree withered away" (Matthew 21:19, 20).

Jesus made true His claims to power by manifesting His power over death — showing His might over all ages and stages.

Look upon the twelve-year-old girl in the house of Jairus, cold in death, and see how Jesus proved His power over death, when "all wept and bewailed her," Jesus said: "She is not dead, but sleepeth."

> And they laughed him to scorn, knowing that she was dead. And he put them all out, and took her by the hand, and called, saying, Maid, arise. And her spirit came again straightway: and he commanded to give her meat. And her parents were astonished: but he charged them that they should tell no man what was done (Luke 8:53-55). And when he thus had spoken, he cried with a loud voice, Lazarus, come forth. And he that was dead came forth, bound hand and foot with graveclothes: and his face was bound about with a napkin. Jesus saith unto them, Loose him, and let him go (John 11:43, 44).

"Our Saviour, Jesus Christ, who hath abolished death, and hath brought life and immortality to light" (I Timothy 9:10).

In the road that led to and from the little town of Nain, a young man was dead and was being carried to the graveyard — and Jesus

> . . . came and touched the bier: and they that bare him stood still, And he said, Young man, I say unto thee, Arise. And he that was dead sat up, and began to speak. And he delivered him to his mother. And there came a fear on all: and they glorified God, saying, That a great prophet is risen up among us; and, That God hath visited his people (Luke 7:14-16).

As one has written: "A picture of that happy Day when the same divine hand shall touch all the biers of all the ransomed dead — and some shall be delivered to mothers, and friend to friend, and loved ones to loved ones, to part no more."

In Bethany, a loved one dead and buried — and decomposition had set in. Jesus said: "Where have ye laid him? . . . . Take ye away the stone . . . . Lazarus, come forth . . . . and he that was dead came forth" (John 11:39-44). After such manifestations of His power over death, He had the authority to say: "Marvel not at this: for the hour is coming, in which all that are in the graves shall hear his voice, and shall come forth" (John 5:28, 29).

Jesus had power over demons.

We read of a son who had one demon:

> And, behold, a man of the company cried out, saying, Master, I beseech thee, look upon my son: for he is mine only child. And, lo, a spirit taketh him, and he suddenly crieth out; and it teareth him that he foameth again, and bruising him hardly departeth from him. And I besought thy disciples to cast him out; and they could not. And Jesus answering said, O faithless and perverse generation, how long shall I be with you, and suffer you? Bring thy son hither. And as he was yet a coming, the devil threw him down, and tare him. And Jesus rebuked the unclean spirit, and healed the child, and delivered him again to his father (Luke 9:38-42).

We read of a woman who had seven demons: "Mary Magdalene out of whom went seven devils" (Luke 8:2). Well, had it been seventy times seven, the result would have been the same.

We read of a man with a legion of demons — "A certain man which had demons a long time . . . And he said, Legion, because many demons were entered into him." At the command of Christ "then went the demons out of the man, and entered into the swine; and the herd ran violently down a steep place into the lake and were choked" (Luke 8:22, 33). Mark tells us that "there were about two thousand." What awful demon power possessed that afflicted man! Yet, as one servant of Christ has taught us, at the "permit" of the Commander of angels, men, and demons, these demons departed and never returned. Even the lowest of animal creation obey Christ's behest, showing that the power Jesus claimed for Himself was not borrowed or delegated, but inherent — "at *this* word" (Matthew 8:16), proving Jesus to be God over all (Romans 9:5).

Jesus had power over Hades and the spirit world:

> I am he that liveth, and was dead; and, behold, I am alive for evermore, Amen; and have the keys of hell and of death (Revelation 1:18).
> And to the angel of the church in Philadelphia write; These things saith he that is holy, he that is true, he that hath the key of David, he that openeth, and no man shutteth; and shutteth, and no man openeth (Revelation 3:7).

"Jesus who can cast into Hades, seal up Hades, and deliver from Hades says to each humble believer 'Fear not.'" No soul trusting in His precious blood can ever, by any means, be found in Hades.

For Himself, Jesus claimed a —

V. SUPERNATURAL MISSION AND MESSAGE

> The thief cometh not, but for to steal, and to kill, and to destroy: I am come that they might have life, and that they might have it more abundantly (John 10:10).
> For the Son of man is come to seek and to save that which was lost (Luke 19:10).
> And as Moses lifted up the serpent in the wilderness, even so must the Son of man be lifted up (John 3:14).

Thus we see that definite and distinct was the knowledge of Jesus as to His wisdom to redeem the world. "Jesus saith unto him, I am the way, the truth, and the life: no man cometh unto the Father, but by me" (John 14:6).

Jesus claimed to be truth itself — expressing and manifesting *creative* truth, *social* truth, *redemptive* truth, *eternal* truth. And along with these assertions, Jesus claimed infallibility. "Heaven and earth shall pass away, but my words shall not pass away" (Matthew 24:35).

As a teacher, Jesus left behind no interrogation points — and gave the humbler virtues crowns of gold, making alien skies friendly.

The masterminds of the ages — searching, scrutinizing, sifting, studying His messages — have never diminished His teaching, never exhausted it. They cannot add to nor subtract one word from what He said.

For Himself, Jesus claimed to have —

VI. SUPERNATURAL WISDOM

> Nathanael saith unto him, Whence knowest thou me? Jesus answered and said unto him, Before that Philip called thee, when thou wast under the fig tree, I saw thee (John 1:48).

He claimed and manifested the penetrative wisdom which enabled Him to read the human heart.

> But Jesus did not commit himself unto them, because he knew all men, and needed not that any should testify of man: for he knew what was in man (John 2:24, 25).
> And Jesus knowing their thoughts said, Wherefore think ye evil in your hearts? (Matthew 9:4).
> But there are some of you that believe not. For Jesus knew from the beginning who they were that believed not, and who should betray him (John 6:64).

Jesus penetrated the secret wonders of Nicodemus. No soldier, He knew all soldiers. He knew the double life of the woman of Sychar—her five husbands and "all that ever she did" (John 4:29).

Not stamped with the imprint of the schools, He knew all scholars. He knew the betrayal thoughts of Judas. "For he knew who should betray him; therefore said he, Ye are not all clean" (John 13:11).

Before Jesus' death, His disciples looked Him in the face and said: "Now are we sure that thou knowest all things, and needest not that any man should ask thee: by this we believe that thou camest forth from God" (John 16:30). Truly, in Jesus, "are hid all the treasures of wisdom and knowledge" (Colossians 2:3).

Jesus knew the end from the beginning. Jesus knew men's thoughts afar off. To Jesus the black midnight was as the brightest noonday. And every *truth* uttered by the wisest of men in all realms in the last nineteen hundred years, in realms scientific, in realms geological, in realms psychological, in realms theological, in realms sociological, in any realm, in all realms, is rooted like a rainbow in something Jesus said.

Jesus claimed —

VII. Power to Forgive Sins

No man who ever lived, no scholar, no philosopher, no preacher, no reformer, can truthfully say: "I can forgive sins." But Jesus could and did claim that power. "But that ye may know that the Son of man hath power on earth to forgive sins, (then saith he to the sick of the palsy,) Arise, take up thy bed, and go unto thine house" (Matthew 9:6). "Jesus . . . said unto her . . . hath no man condemned thee? She said, No man, Lord. And Jesus said unto her, Neither do I condemn thee: go, and sin no more" (John 8:10, 11). "And, behold, they brought to him a man sick of the palsy, lying on a bed: and Jesus seeing their faith said unto the sick of the palsy; Son, be of good cheer; thy sins be forgiven thee" (Matthew 9:2).

"God for Christ's sake hath forgiven you" (Ephesians 4:32). Through Jesus, who forgives sins, we have forgiveness.

> In whom we have redemption through his blood, even the
> forgiveness of sins (Colossians 1:14).

Jesus claimed to have —

VIII. Power to Impart Eternal Life

Not only could Jesus forgive the sins of men, but He could give to the soul eternal life — a life which no flood could drown, no fire consume, no disease could eliminate, no treachery violate, no death destroy. "For as the Father hath life in himself; so hath he given to the Son to have life in himself" (John 5:26).

In speaking of His own life, He said: "No man taketh it from me, but I lay it down of myself. I have power to lay it down,

and I have power to take it again. This commandment have I
received of my Father" (John 10:18). But greater comfort we
have in remembering these words:

> My sheep hear my voice, and I know them, and they
> follow me: And I give unto them eternal life; and they
> shall never perish, neither shall any man pluck them out
> of my hand. My Father, which gave them me, is greater
> than all; and no man is able to pluck them out of my
> Father's hand (John 10:27-29).

Jesus claimed —

IX. EQUALITY WITH GOD

"I and my Father are one" (John 10:30).

It was an equivocal claim of absolute equality. Equality — not
of sympathy. Equality — not in disposition, but in essence of
Being.

In Jesus, the mind of God thought out.

In Jesus, the heart of God throbbed out and loved out.

In Jesus, the hands of God reached out and worked out.

In Jesus, the feet of God walked out.

In Jesus, the eyes of God looked out — sometimes weepingly.

In Jesus, the ears of God listened out.

The character of Jesus is the *all* of God.

Being God, Jesus is God eternally and inherently — without
cause, without beginning, without mutation, without measure,
without evil. He was no emanation, no effulgence, no symbol,
no mere reflection, but *was* God, *is* God, and *will be* God
forevermore.

> No man hath seen God at any time; the only begotten
> Son, which is in the bosom of the Father, he hath de-
> clared him (John 1:18).
> Jesus saith unto him, Have I been so long time with you,
> and yet hast thou not known me, Philip? he that hath
> seen me hath seen the Father; and how sayest thou then,
> Shew us the Father? (John 14:9).

"Any rational being with a brain to think and a bosom to throb,
in his heart of hearts, must conclude that Christ was, and is, and
ever shall be God — to which be glory eternal." Thus Christ is
the central, supreme, and superlative fact of the ages. Moreover,
Jesus claimed equal honor with God. "That all men should

honour the Son, even as they honour the Father. He that honoureth not the Son honoureth not the Father which hath sent him" (John 5:23).

Jesus claimed —

X. DOMINION OVER MAN

And this claim was an exclusive claim. "If ye love me, keep my commandments" (John 14:15).

Repeatedly Jesus said: "Follow me."

Insistently Jesus said: "Follow me."

He called upon men — all men — to leave all and follow Him — declaring that even the closest of domestic ties and the demands of remunerative business must not stand in the way of allegiance to Him.

Note His words:

> If any man come to me, and hate not his father, and mother, and wife, and children, and brethren, and sisters, yea, and his own life also, he can not be my disciple (Luke 14:26).
> So likewise, whosoever he be of you that forsaketh not all that he hath, he can not be my disciple (Luke 14:33).
> And as Jesus passed forth from thence, he saw a man, named Matthew, sitting at the receipt of custom: and he saith unto him, Follow me. And he arose, and followed him (Matthew 9:9).

Jesus claimed —

XI. EXCLUSIVE AND PECULIAR KNOWLEDGE OF GOD

Neither knoweth any man the Father, save the Son, and he to whomsoever the Son will reveal him (Matthew 11:27).

Speaking in the temple Jesus cried: "Ye both know me, and ye know whence I am: and I am not come of myself, but he that sent me is true, whom ye know not. But I know him: for I am from him, and he hath sent me" (John 7:28, 29).

Never at any time, never anywhere, does Jesus identify His relationship to the Father with that of the disciples — or anybody else. "As the Father knoweth me, even so know I the Father" (John 10:15). Only Jesus is the answer to the question of Job: "Canst thou by searching find out God? canst thou find out the Almighty unto perfection?" (Job 11:7).

Jesus claimed the —

XII. Right to Receive Worship

Jesus accepted worship from men, women, and children —
without any demur. No other man could ever make such a claim
without stirring up abhorrence and awakening the repulsions of
multitudes. Out of the sixty times worship is mentioned in the
New Testament, fifteen times it is distinctly ascribed *to* and
accepted *by* the Lord Jesus.

Jesus despises any patronage men offer. Jesus demands of
men worship. The Apostle Peter refused worship from Cornelius,
saying: "Stand up; I myself also am a man" (Acts 10:25, 26).

Paul and Barnabas refused worshipful sacrifice from the priests
of Jupiter and the people. Tearing their clothes, they ran in
among the people, crying: "Sirs, why do ye these things? We
also are men of like passions . . . . . ye should turn from these
vanities to the living God" (Acts 14:11).

When the Apostle John "fell down to worship before the feet"
even of an angel, he was at once corrected with the words: "See
thou do it not; for I am thy fellow servant — worship God"
(Revelation 22:8, 9).

Take note of a few of these instances of worship accepted:

> And when they were come into the house, they saw the
> young child with Mary his mother, and fell down, and
> worshipped him: and when they had opened their treas-
> ures, they presented unto him gifts; gold, and frankin-
> cense, and myrrh (Matthew 2:11).
> And, behold, there came a leper and worshipped him,
> saying, Lord, if thou wilt, thou canst make me clean
> (Matthew 8:2).
> While he spake these things unto them, behold, there
> came a certain ruler, and worshipped him, saying, My
> daughter is even now dead: but come and lay thy hand
> upon her, and she shall live (Matthew 9:18).
> Then they that were in the ship came and worshipped
> him, saying, Of a truth thou art the Son of God (Mat-
> thew 14:33).

In the Temple, the children cried singingly: "Hosanna." His
enemies, following Him as hounds follow a stag, said: "Stop
these children! They are giving praise to you — praise that belongs to God. Don't let them worship thee. Worship belongs

to God." Jesus answered their malicious criticisms with these words: "I tell you that, if these should hold their peace, the stones would immediately cry out" (Luke 19:40).

After His resurrection the women "came and held Him by the feet, and *worshipped* Him" (Matthew 28:9).

The eleven disciples, at their first meeting after the resurrection, "worshipped him" — their glorious risen Saviour (Matthew 28:17).

At the Ascension the company of the disciples "*worshipped* Him and returned to Jerusalem with great joy" — worship and joy being twins.

After the eventful eight days, when Jesus showed His pierced hands and wounded side to Thomas, Thomas uttered the worshipping words which continue to be used by many redeemed lips — "My Lord and my God" (John 20:25).

Never for any second of any minute of any hour of any day did Jesus acknowledge the least impropriety in receiving adoration and worship. Always, without any apology, without any sense of impropriety, Jesus accepted the worship men gave. The blessed Scriptures make clear that the worship which neither men nor angels dared to accept, Jesus, God manifest in the flesh (I Timothy 3:16), the keynote of all the ransomed and angels in heaven, freely welcomed, because such homage fulfilled the injunction, "*Worship God.*"

Jesus claimed —

XIII. OMNIPRESENCE

Go ye therefore, and teach all nations, baptizing them in the name of the Father, and of the Son, and of the Holy Ghost: Teaching them to observe all things whatsoever I have commanded you: and, lo, I am with you alway, even unto the end of the world (Matthew 28:19, 20).

"With you *always.*"

Thus God calls for a world-wide proclamation. And this world-wide proclamation is vitalized by a world-wide presence, which is possessed of a world-wide power.

Jesus is everywhere. The wisest minds of men can think of and state no place where He is not.

Let your conversation be without covetousness; and be content with such things as ye have: for he hath said, I will never leave thee, nor forsake thee (Hebrews 13:5). Jesus answered and said unto him, If a man love me, he will keep my words: and my Father will love him, and we will come unto him, and make our abode with him (John 14:23).

Jesus claimed to be the —

XIV. JUDGE OF MEN

For the Father judgeth no man, but hath committed all judgment unto the Son (John 5:22).

Jesus claimed to be the judge of all the earth. "All judgment." Luke, in the book of Acts, testifies to the truth of this claim when he writes this God-breathed Scripture: "God . . . hath appointed a day, in which he will judge the world in righteousness by that man whom he hath ordained; whereof he hath given assurance unto all men in that he hath raised him from the dead" (Acts 17:30, 31).

And God, through the Apostle Paul, testifies to Jesus' judgment claims in these words:

For there is no respect of persons with God. For as many as have sinned without law shall also perish without law: and as many as have sinned in the law shall be judged by the law; In the day when God shall judge the secrets of men by Jesus Christ according to my gospel (Romans 2:11, 12, 16).

All the seven things which God alone can do are attributed to Jesus Christ — creating, upholding all things, forgiving sins, giving eternal life, transforming human bodies, raising the dead, judging all men.

"Judging all men!" As to that most awful attribute, we give Scripture proof: "For the Father judgeth no man, but hath committed all judgment unto the Son" (John 5:22).

Marvel not at this: for the hour is coming, in the which all that are in the graves shall hear his voice, And shall come forth; they that have done good, unto the resurrection of life; and they that have done evil, unto the resurrection of damnation. I can of mine own self do nothing: as I hear, I judge: and my judgment is just; because I seek not mine own will, but the will of the Father which hath sent me (John 5:28-30).

> I charge thee therefore before God, and the Lord Jesus
> Christ, who shall judge the quick and the dead at his
> appearing and his kingdom (II Timothy 4:1).

To Jesus, who said to His disciples, "Judge not that ye be not judged" (Matthew 7:1), is committed the judgment of all men and all nations, for before Him, Son of Man without sin and Son of God with power, shall be gathered all nations — and He shall separate them as a shepherd divideth his sheep from the goats (Matthew 23).

Jesus claimed that He was —

XV. CALVARY-LIFTED AND THE LIFTER

David, whose God was the Lord, testified: "He brought me up also out of an horrible pit, out of the miry clay, and set my feet upon a rock, and established my goings" (Psalm 40:2).

But Jesus, both Lord and Christ (Acts 2:36), Lord also of the Sabbath (Luke 6:5), said: "And I, if I be lifted up from the earth, will draw all men unto me. This he said, signifying what death he should die" (John 12:32, 33).

"All men." That does not mean that all individuals, but men of all races shall be drawn to Him. Jesus appeals to all *races* — no matter what the color of the skin. Not every individual, but all races of men — Greeks, Jews, Romans, Scythians, French, English, German, Russian, Japanese, Chinese, Americans, of all nations. His *"whosoever"* breaks down all partition walls, all class, all racial barriers.

Buddha tried to lift India. Confucius tried to lift China. Zoroaster tried to lift Persia. Plato tried to lift Athens. Caesar tried to lift Rome. Savonarola, whose dying whispers broke in thunders over the Dark Ages, trying to lift Italy, was throttled with a chain and burned to ashes. God reached down from the skies, took those ashes and flung them all over Europe. Wherever those ashes fell, the earth shook. Amid this shaking, Luther tried to lift Germany. Knox tried to lift Scotland. Washington tried to lift America. Each one succeeded only partially.

But Christ claimed, "If I be lifted up, I will draw *all* men unto me." Twenty centuries vindicate His claims. And this is true though, during the days of His flesh on earth, He was an unwelcome visitor in the synagogue, an intruder in the Sanhedrin, a disturber of the peace of the State, an unwelcome servitor in the midst of His own people, and a homeless vagrant in the eyes of society. Today, Jesus draws men of all races and nations, though the Pharisees outlawed Him, the Sadducees rejected Him, though His kindred spurned Him, society rejected Him, the State crucified Him.

Jesus claimed He would —

XVI. MAKE A PERSONAL RETURN TO EARTH

"I will come again" (John 14:31).

And we should be found daily "looking for that Blessed Hope and the glorious appearing of the great God and our Saviour, Jesus Christ" (Titus 2:13).

Grand the fact in history that Christ Jesus, the Lord of Glory, has been in the world. The most important fact of the present is that Jesus is now in heaven making intercession for us. The greatest prophesied event of the future is that Jesus is coming again.

The Lord Jesus, who so loved the world that He died for it, whom having not seen we love, will come down out of heaven in *person* — the first time He has shown *Himself* — in 1900 years, except to Paul, to Stephen, to John at Patmos. Just as surely as Christ was God incarnate, just as surely as Christ's death was redemptive — as He "died for our sins according to the Scriptures" (I Corinthians 15:3), so surely will He make good His claim to return to earth — bodily, visibly, gloriously.

Just as surely as Christ's bodily resurrection was evidence of Christ's authority, the test of Christ's deity, the complement of His Calvary sacrifice, so will Christ come back to earth again to take over the affairs of the world, and complete that which He began on Calvary's cross — a coming back which looks to a conquest of the whole earth. Jesus will make real His promise to return by coming back, by raising the righteous dead, by enabling the living Christians to be "caught up together with them to meet the Lord in the air" (I Thessalonians 4). Jesus is coming back to reign in righteousness. "The same Lord Jesus who showed Himself alive after his passion, by many infallible proofs" (Acts

1:3), who was "taken up from you into heaven, shall so come in like manner as ye have seen him go into heaven" (Acts 1:9-11). Referring to the fig tree as a sign, the Lord Jesus said:

> So ye in like manner, when ye shall see these things come to pass know that it is nigh even at the doors (Mark 13:29).

According to the present fulfillment of prophetic signs, Jesus' hand must be on the door knob — ready to swing the doors open.

Jesus "shall descend from heaven." For two thousand years the heavens have been closed. They opened. They opened when Jesus came to Bethlehem, when He was buried in baptism in Jordan's waters, when He was transfigured on the Mount, when He ascended. God opened the heavenly doors to welcome Jesus back. Then God closed the doors. But they will open toward earth again when Jesus returns to earth.

> Beloved, now are we the sons of God, and it doth not yet appear what we shall be: but we know that, when he shall appear, we shall be like him; for we shall see him as he is. And every man that hath this hope in him purifieth himself, even as he is pure (I John 3:2, 3).

"Him, as He is!"

*Centuries of Prophecy Fulfilled
in One Day*

> But all this was done, that the scriptures of the pro-
> phets might be fulfilled (Matthew 26:56).

From some old college classroom notes, from the ransacking of some musty religious periodicals which I have kept for years, from some remembrances of some portions of sermons on prophecy I heard years ago, from some of my own searching of the Scriptures, I have prepared this message — a message of many prophecies in the Old Testament on the betrayal, the trial, the death, the burial of Jesus Christ. Yes. And prophecies from different prophets five centuries apart, from 1000 B.C. to 500 B.C., fulfilled within twenty-four hours on the awesome day of Christ's crucifixion on Calvary.

I. Sold for Thirty (30) Pieces of Silver

Prophecy: About 500 B.C., Zechariah had prophesied toward the cross, and had said: "And I said unto them, If ye think good, give me my price; and if not, forbear. So they weighed for my price thirty pieces of silver" (Zechariah 11:12).

Fulfillment: "Then one of the twelve, called Judas Iscariot, went unto the chief priests, and said unto them, What will ye give me and I will deliver him unto you? And they covenanted with him for thirty pieces of silver" (Matthew 26:14, 15).

II. Betrayed by a Friend

Prophecy: "For it was not an enemy that reproached me; then I could have borne it: . . . . But it was thou, a man mine equal, my guide, and mine acquaintance. We took sweet counsel together, and walked unto the house of God in company" (Psalm 55:12-14).

143

"Yea, mine own familiar friend, in whom I trusted, which did eat of my bread, hath lifted up his heel against me" (Psalm 41:9).

"And one shall say unto him, What are these wounds in thine hands? Then he shall answer, Those with which I was wounded in the house of my friends" (Zechariah 13:6).

Fulfillment: "And forthwith he (Judas) came to Jesus, and said, Hail, master; and kissed him. And Jesus said unto him, Friend, wherefore art thou come? Then came they, and laid hands on Jesus, and took him" (Matthew 26:49, 50).

"Men and brethren, this scripture must needs have been fulfilled, which the Holy Ghost by the mouth of David spake before concerning Judas, which was guide to them that took Jesus" (Acts 1:16).

"I speak not of you all: I know whom I have chosen: but that the scripture may be fulfilled, He that eateth bread with me hath lifted up his heel against me. Now I tell you before it come, that, when it is come to pass, ye may believe that I am he" (John 13:18, 19).

III. THE MONEY CAST TO THE POTTER

Prophecy: "And the Lord said unto me, Cast it unto the potter: a goodly price that I was prised at of them. And I took the thirty pieces of silver, and cast them to the potter in the house of the Lord" (Zechariah 11:13).

Fulfillment: "And he (Judas) cast down the pieces of silver in the temple, and departed, and went and hanged himself. And the chief priests took the silver pieces . . . . And they took counsel, and bought with them the potter's field" (Matthew 27:5-7).

"They took counsel, and bought with them the potter's field, to bury strangers in. Wherefore that field was called, The field of blood, unto this day. Then was fulfilled that which was spoken by Jeremy the prophet, saying, And they took the thirty pieces of silver, the price of him that was valued, whom they of the children of Israel did value; And gave them for the potter's field, as the Lord appointed me" (Matthew 27:7-10).

Note that in prophecy and fulfillment, we find stated that (1) It was silver. (2) There were thirty pieces. (3) They were thrown down. (4) They were cast down in the house of the Lord. (5) The money was used to purchase the potters' field.

IV. THE DISCIPLES FORSOOK HIM

Prophecy: "Smite the shepherd and the sheep shall be scattered" (Zechariah 13:7).

Fulfillment: "All the disciples forsook him and fled" (Matthew 26:56).

"And Jesus answered and said unto them, Are ye come out, as against a thief, with swords and with staves to take me? I was daily with you in the temple teaching, and ye took me not: but the scriptures must be fulfilled. And they all forsook him, and fled" (Mark 14:48-50).

V. ACCUSED BY FALSE WITNESSES

Prophecy: "False witnesses did rise up; they laid to my charge things that I knew not" (Psalm 35:11).

Fulfillment: "Now the chief priests, and elders, and all the council, sought false witness against Jesus, to put him to death . . . . At last came two false witnesses" (Matthew 26:59, 60).

How they twisted the words of Jesus!

See John 2:21: "But he spake of the temple of his body." And put over against that Matthew 26:61: "And said, This fellow said, I am able to destroy the temple of God, and to build it in three days." And Mark 14:58: "We heard him say, I will destroy this temple that is made with hands, and within three days I will build another made without hands."

VI. SMITTEN AND SPIT UPON

Prophecy: "I gave my back to the smiters, and my cheeks to them that plucked off the hair: I hid not my face from shame and spitting" (Isaiah 50:6).

Fulfillment: "Then did they spit in his face, and buffeted him; and others smote him with the palms of their hands" (Matthew 26:67, 68).

Note here the details that correspond in both prophecy and fulfillment: (1) He was to be smitten. (2) He was to be smitten on the face (as well as the other parts of the body).

In Luke 22:64: "And when they had blindfolded him, they struck him on the face, and asked him saying, Prophesy who it is that smote thee!"

(3) He was to be spit upon, and (4) He was to be spit upon in the face.

VII. Dumb Before His Accusers

Prophecy: "He was oppressed and he was afflicted, yet he opened not his mouth; he is brought as a lamb to the slaughter, and as a sheep before her shearers is dumb, so he openeth not his mouth" (Isaiah 53:7).

Fulfillment: "And when he was accused of the chief priests and elders he answered nothing. Then Pilate said unto him, Hearest thou not how many things they witness against thee? *And he answered Him to never a word,* insomuch that the governor marveled greatly" (Matthew 27:12-14).

Reviled but He reviled not again!

VIII. Wounded and Bruised

Prophecy: "He was wounded for our transgressions, he was bruised for our iniquities. The chastisement of our peace was upon him; and with his stripes we are healed" (Isaiah 53:5).

Fulfillment: "When he had scourged Jesus, he delivered him to be crucified. And when they had platted a crown of thorns they put it upon his head" (Matthew 27:26, 29).

In this bruised Christ the arts have awaked in truth and beauty. In Him law and love, justice and mercy are reconciled by sacrifice. In Him religion cleansed of superstition, prejudice and pride.

> My sins laid open to the rod
> The back which from the law was free;
> And the eternal Son of God
> Received the stripes once due to me.
>
> Nor beam was in His eye, nor mote,
> Nor laid to Him was any blame;
> And yet His cheeks for me were smote —
> The cheeks that never blushed for shame.
>
> I pierced those sacred hands and feet
> That never touched or walked in sin;
> I broke the heart that only beat
> The souls of sinful men to win.

> That sponge of vinegar and gall
>> Was placed by me upon His tongue;
> And when derision mocked His call
>> I stood that mocking crowd among.

> And yet His blood was shed for me,
>> To be of sin the double cure;
> And balm there flows from Calvary's tree
>> That heals my guilt and makes me pure.

IX. HIS THIRST

Prophecy: "My strength is dried up like a potsherd, and my tongue cleaveth to my jaws; and thou hast brought me into the dust of death" (Psalm 22:15).

Fulfillment: "I thirst" (John 19:28).

X. FELL UNDER THE CROSS

Prophecy: "My knees are weak through fasting; and my flesh faileth of fatness" (Psalm 109:24).

Fulfillment: "And he, bearing his cross, went forth" (John 19:17). "They laid hold upon one Simon . . . and on him they laid the cross, that he might bear it after Jesus" (Luke 23:26).

Evidently the Lord was so weak that His knees gave way under the weight of the heavy cross. So they had to put it on another.

XI. HANDS AND FEET PIERCED

Prophecy: "For dogs have compassed me: the assembly of the wicked have inclosed me: they pierced my hands and my feet" (Psalm 22:16).

Fulfillment: "And when they were come to the place, which is called Calvary, there they crucified him" (Luke 23:33).

Christ was crucified in the customary Roman manner, the hands and feet being pierced by huge spikes which fastened the body to the wooden cross. John 20:25, 27: ". . . Except I shall see in his hands the print of the nails, and put my finger into the print of the nails . . . . Then said he (Jesus) to Thomas, Reach hither thy finger, and behold my hands; and reach hither thy hand, and thrust it into my side."

XII. CRUCIFIED WITH THIEVES

Prophecy: "He was numbered with the transgressors" (Isaiah 53:12).

Fulfillment: "And with him they crucify two thieves; the one on his right hand, and the other on his left. And the scripture was fulfilled, which saith, And he was numbered with the transgressors" (Mark 15:27, 28).

The Apostle Peter speaks, "Who his own self bare our sins in his own body on the tree, that we, being dead to sins, should live unto righteousness: by whose stripes ye were healed" (I Peter 2:24).

Calling the cross of Christ a tree, we say that there were three trees on Calvary that awesome day. On the three trees, three men died. One died *for* sin. That was Jesus. One died *in* sin. That was the impenitent thief. One died saved *from* sin. That was the penitent thief.

One died in love. That was Jesus. One died in scorn. That was the impenitent thief. One died in faith. That was the penitent thief.

One died a benefactor. That was *Jesus.* One died a blasphemer. That was the impenitent thief. One died a believer. That was the penitent thief.

One tree was the tree of *redemption.* That was the tree on which Jesus died. One tree was the tree of *rejection.* That was the tree on which the impenitent thief died. One tree was the tree of *reception.* That was the tree on which the penitent thief died.

XIII. Prayer for Persecutors

Prophecy: "He made intercession for the transgressors" (Isaiah 53:12).

Fulfillment: "Then said Jesus, Father, forgive them; for they know not what they do" (Luke 23:34).

This was not a prayer for God to wink at the sin of ignorance. Nor was it a prayer for God to grant a blanket pardon for His crucifiers. And it was not a prayer for God to thrust forgiveness upon men who did not want forgiveness.

XIV. People Shook Their Heads

Prophecy: "I became also a reproach to them: when they looked upon me they shaked their heads" (Psalm 109:25).

"All they that see me laugh me to scorn: they shoot out the lip, they shake the head, saying, He trusted on the Lord that He would deliver him: let Him deliver him, seeing He delighted in Him" (Psalm 22:7, 8).

Fulfillment: "And they that passed by, reviled him, wagging their heads" (Matthew 27:39).

Simeon: "Yes, a sword shall pierce through thine own soul also." "There stood by the cross of Jesus his mother" (John 19:25).

XV. PEOPLE RIDICULED HIM

Prophecy: "They say, He trusted on the Lord that He would deliver him: let him deliver him, seeing he delighted in him" (Psalm 22:8).

Fulfillment: "Likewise also the chief priests mocked him with the scribes and elders, said, He trusted in God; let Him deliver him now, if he will have him" (Matthew 27:41-43).

XVI. PEOPLE ASTONISHED

Prophecy: "They look and stare upon me" (Psalm 22:17).

Fulfillment: "Sitting down they watched him there" (Matthew 27:36). "And the people stood beholding" (Luke 23:35). "And all the people that came together to that sight, beholding the things which were done, smote their breasts, and returned" (Luke 23:48).

XVII. GARMENTS PARTED AND LOTS CAST

Prophecy: "They part my garments among them, and cast lots upon my vesture" (Psalm 22:18).

Fulfillment: "Then the soldiers, when they had crucified Jesus, took his garments, and made four parts, to every soldier a part; and also his coat: now the coat was without seam, woven from the top throughout. They said therefore among themselves, Let us not rend it, but cast lots for it, whose it shall be: that the scripture might be fulfilled, which saith, They parted my raiment among them, and for my vesture they did cast lots" (John 19:23, 24).

How exact the inspired prophecy! The garments were to be *parted* among them, but the vesture was to be *awarded* to one by *lots.* These were statements that would appear almost contradictory unless explained by the record of the scene at the cross.

XVIII. His Forsaken Cry

"Psalm 22 our Lord appropriated to himself." This Psalm was the subject of His meditation in His dying agony.

Prophecy: "My God, my God, why hast thou forsaken me?" (Psalm 22:1). "In that hour the serpent's heel was bruised."

Fulfillment: "Jesus cried with a loud voice, saying, "My God, my God, why hast thou forsaken me?" (Matthew 27:46). Also: "And at the ninth hour Jesus cried with a loud voice, saying, Eloi, Eloi, lama sabachthani! which is, being interpreted, My God, my God, why hast thou forsaken me?" (Mark 15:34).

This was the only time Jesus ever called His Father, "God."

> Well might the sun in darkness hide,
> And shut his glories in,
> When Christ, the mighty Maker, died,
> For man, the creature's sin.

XIX. Gall and Vinegar Given Him

Prophecy: "They gave me also gall for my meat; and in my thirst they gave me vinegar to drink" (Psalm 69:21).

Fulfillment: "After this, Jesus . . . saith, I THIRST. Now there was set a vessel full of vinegar: and they filled a spunge with vinegar, and put it upon hyssop, and put it to his mouth" (John 19:28, 29).

XX. Committed Himself to God

Prophecy: Into thine hand I commit my spirit" (Psalm 31:5).

Fulfillment: "And when Jesus had cried with a loud voice, he said, Father, into thy hands I commend my spirit" (Luke 23:46).

XXI. Friends Stood Afar Off

Prophecy: "My lovers and my friends stand aloof from my sore; and my kinsmen stand afar off" (Psalm 38:11).

Fulfillment: "And all his acquaintance, and the women that followed him from Galilee, stood afar off, beholding these things" (Luke 23:49).

XXII. Bones Not Broken

Prophecy: "He keepeth all his bones: not one of them is broken" (Psalm 34:20).

Fulfillment: "When they came to Jesus, and saw that he was dead already, they brake not his legs. For these things were done that the scripture should be fulfilled, A bone of him shall not be broken" (John 19:33, 36).

XXIII. HEART BROKEN

Prophecy: "My heart is like wax; it is melted in the midst of my bowels" (Psalm 22:14).

Fulfillment: "But one of the soldiers with a spear pierced his side, and forthwith came there out blood and water" (John 19:34).

"Blood and water running out of the pierced side evidence that the heart had literally burst."

XXIV. HIS SIDE PIERCED

Prophecy: "They shall look upon me whom they have pierced" (Zechariah 12:10).

Fulfillment: "And one of the soldiers with a spear pierced his side" (John 19:34).

"And he that saw it bare record, and his record is *true;* and he knoweth that he saith true, that ye might believe" (John 19:35).

"And again another scripture saith, They shall look on him whom they pierced" (John 19:37).

XXV. DARKNESS OVER THE LAND

Prophecy: "And it shall come to pass in that day, saith the Lord God, that I will cause the sun to go down at noon, and I will darken the earth in the clear day" (Amos 8:9).

Fulfillment: "Now from the sixth hour there was darkness over all the land unto the ninth hour" (Matthew 27:45).

The Jews reckoned twelve hours from sunrise to sunset. When then was the *sixth hour?* The *sixth hour* was *noon* and the *ninth hour* was *three* in the afternoon.

Midnight came down at midday and pushed noonday, with her bright and resplendent garments, off the throne of the universe — and spread black garments over all the earth.

Thus the prophecy made nearly eight hundred years before Christ was fulfilled.

XXVI. Jesus Died Willingly

Prophecy: "Then said I, Lo, I come: in the volume of the book it is written of me, I delight to do thy will, O my God: yea, thy law is within my heart" (Psalm 40:7, 8).

Fulfillment: "I am the good shepherd: the good shepherd giveth his life for the sheep. But he that is an hireling, and not the shepherd, whose own the sheep are not, seeth the wolf coming, and leaveth the sheep, and fleeth: and the wolf catcheth them, and scattereth the sheep. The hireling fleeth, because he is an hireling, and careth not for the sheep. I am the good shepherd, and know my sheep, and am known of mine. As the Father knoweth me, even so know I the Father: and I lay down my life for the sheep. And other sheep I have, which are not of this fold: them also I must bring, and they shall hear my voice; and there shall be one fold, and one shepherd. Therefore doth my Father love me, because I lay down my life, that I might take it again" (John 10:11-17).

XXVII. Jesus Was Hated Without a Cause

Prophecy: "They that hate me without a cause are more than the hairs of mine head: they that would destroy me, being mine enemies wrongfully, are mighty: then I restored that which I took not away" (Psalm 69:4).

Fulfillment: "But this cometh to pass, that the word might be fulfilled that is written in their law, They hated me without a cause" (John 15:25).

XXVIII. Jesus' Visage Was Marred

Prophecy: "As many were astonied at thee; his visage was so marred more than any man, and his form more than the sons of men" (Isaiah 52:14).

Fulfillment: "And when they had platted a crown of thorns, they put it upon his head, and a reed in his right hand: and they bowed the knee before him, and mocked him, saying, Hail, King of the Jews! And they spit upon him, and took the reed, and smote him on the head" (Matthew 27:29, 30).

XXIX. Jesus Rejected by His Own

Prophecy: "I was a reproach among all mine enemies, but especially among my neighbours, and a fear to mine acquaintance: they that did see me without fled from me" (Psalm 31:11).

Fulfillment: "He came unto his own, and his own received him not" (John 1:11).

XXX. JUDAS DIED. LAND DESOLATE

Prophecy: "Let their habitation be desolate; and let none dwell in their tents" (Psalm 69:25).

Fulfillment: "Men and brethren, this scripture must needs have been fulfilled, which the Holy Ghost by the mouth of David spake before concerning Judas, which was guide to them that took Jesus. For he was numbered with us, and had obtained part of this ministry. Now this man purchased a field with the reward of iniquity; and falling headlong, he burst asunder in the midst, and all his bowels gushed out. And it was known unto all the dwellers at Jerusalem; insomuch as that field is called in their proper tongue, Aceldama, that is to say, The field of blood. For it is written in the book of Psalms, Let his habitation be desolate, and let no man dwell therein: and his bishoprick let another take" (Acts 1:16-20.

XXXI. BURIED IN A RICH MAN'S TOMB

Prophecy: "He made his grave with the wicked, and with the rich in his death" (Isaiah 53:9).

Fulfillment: "When the even was come, there came a *rich* man of Arimathaea, named Joseph, who also himself was Jesus' disciple: He went to Pilate, and begged the body of Jesus . . . . And when Joseph had taken the body, he wrapped it in a clean linen cloth, And laid it in his own new tomb" (Matthew 27:57-60).

These are quite an array of prophecies. This array of prophecies extends over a long period of time. This array of prophecies was completely fulfilled in one Person. These prophecies were completely fulfilled within the limits of one day. Such truth appeals to every honest mind as one of the undeniable proofs: that the Scripture can be none other than the inspired Word of God. All that the prophets spoke in the years from 1000 B.C. to 500 B.C. came true in one day — *just* as they said, absolutely, literally. What further claim need I, need you, needs anyone, to know assuredly that the Bible is the *Word of God*, inspired in totality? God's Word authenticates itself, firm and unalterable, for it is "fixed in heaven." "Forever, O Lord, thy word is settled in heaven" (Psalm 119:89). God's Word is true and reliable, for it is "true from the beginning." "Thy word is true from the beginning" (Psalm 119:160). God's Word is enlightening and guiding, for it is a "lamp" and a "light" (Psalm 119:105). "Thy word is a lamp unto my feet, and a light unto my path." God's Word is expansive and searching, for it is exceeding broad. "Thy commandment is exceeding broad" (Psalm 119:96). God's Word is divine and wonderful. "Thy testimonies are wonderful" (Psalm 119:129).

To repeat, we say again that such an array of prophecies, such an array of prophecies extending over so long a period of time, such an array of prophecies being so completely fulfilled in *one* Person — and all within the narrow limits of one day — appeals to all honest minds as one of the undeniable proofs that the Scriptures can be none other than the inspired, infallible, inerrant Word of God, and that Jesus of Nazareth, Son of Man without sin, is really the Son of God to whom all power is given in heaven and in earth.

> But these are written, that ye might believe that Jesus is the Christ, the Son of God; and that believing ye might have life through his name (John 20:31).